About the Author

Sadhya has been the Kitchen Administrator at the Cancer Help Centre in Bristol for two years. Her interest in wholefood cooking began twenty odd years ago when her children were small. The family became vegetarian and she started experimenting with macrobiotics and wholefoods.

When the family moved to a remote farmhouse in North Wales she was able to indulge her passion for vegetable gardening and foraging for wild foods. With her husband, she ran a centre in Wales, feeding large numbers of guests from her farmhouse kitchen. When her children left home, she moved to a large commune in Suffolk and for a time was a house mother, preparing vegetarian meals for a hungry building crew. She saw the television programme about the Cancer Help Centre called 'A Gentle Way With Cancer' and the memory stayed with her. Later, visiting Bristol, she came to the centre to see if she could be involved. That day a vacancy had occurred in the kitchen. She was offered a job. Shortly afterwards the position of Kitchen Administrator became available and she filled the vacancy.

The idea for this book came soon afterwards. Patients wanted recipes for the meals that they had enjoyed and it became clear that there was great demand for a book giving practical advice on how to follow the diet along with tasty, interesting recipes. Here it is.

THE BRISTOL RECIPE BOOK

Over 150 recipes from the Cancer Help Kitchen

Sadhya Rippon

Foreword by Penny Brohn

Illustrated by Emma Rippon

CENTURY

LONDON   MELBOURNE   AUCKLAND   JOHANNESBURG

First published in 1987 by Century Hutchinson Ltd,
Brookmount House, 62–65 Chandos Place, Covent Garden,
London WC2N 4NW

Century Hutchinson Australia Pty Ltd
PO Box 496, 16–22 Church Street, Hawthorn, Victoria 3122, Australia

Century Hutchinson New Zealand Limited,
PO Box 40–086, Glenfield, Auckland 10, New Zealand

Century Hutchinson South Africa (Pty) Ltd,
PO Box 337, Bergvlei, 2012 South Africa

Filmset by Deltatype, Ellesmere Port, Cheshire

Printed and bound in Great Britain by
The Guernsey Press Co Ltd,
Guernsey, Channel Islands

British Library Cataloguing in Publication Data
Rippon, Sadhya
The Bristol Recipe Book: over 150 recipes
from the Cancer Help Kitchen.
1. Cancer—Diet therapy—Recipes
I. Title
641.5′631   RC271.D52
ISBN 0–7126–1518–0

Contents

Acknowledgements

My thanks are first to the patients at the Cancer Help Centre. Your enthusiasm for this book kept me at it through the many long evenings at the typewriter. Especial thanks go to the patients who were recipe testers for the book and who tried and adapted the recipes and made many helpful suggestions.

My love and thanks also go to the cooks, past and present, in the kitchen at the Cancer Help Centre, especially Sandipo, Marke, Chris, Helen, James, Pete, Kanksha, Frank, and of course Cas. You're all in this book.

Love, Sadhya.

Foreword

Although diet is only a part of the Bristol Programme it is quite natural that it should loom large in the role that it plays in the lives of our patients. Food means more to us than nutrition. It is a way of comforting ourselves and also a means of celebration. It is a ritual full of blessings, meanings and associations. Any use of nutrition as therapy that does not understand this is doomed to failure. The best dietary advice in the world will not be worth the paper it's written on if it doesn't taste good. Actually, some of the recipes I have tried over the years have tasted remarkably like the paper they were written on, so I for one welcome the arrival of this book.

Visitors to the Cancer Help Centre at Bristol have cause to be grateful for the appointment of Sadhya Rippon to run the kitchen at Grove House. It has to be said by those of us old enough to remember and honest enough to admit it that our first efforts at serving food to our clients were remarkable more for their enthusiastic conviction than any noticeable culinary skills. Mercifully, we soon built up a team of helpers who rectified this and now we are rightly proud of our achievements. The meals that are prepared here so lovingly and carefully, with such imagination and style, have long been admired. Now they are available to everyone.

Thanks to Sadhya's example I am now able to produce meals that even a bunch of fussy teenagers will devour without question and that I can serve up to my friends with pride.

Thank you Sadhya. I hope this is the first of many.

Note
The full Bristol Programme is discussed in the companion to this book, *The Bristol Programme* by Penny Brohn (Century Hutchinson, 1987).

Preface

Right from the early days of the Cancer Help Centre in Bristol many of our friends have been asking for a really comprehensive book on food preparation, which will offer help to anyone wanting to follow our dietary concepts. And so it is with the greatest of pleasure that I am introducing this recipe book to you.

Anyone in the field of natural healing methods is aware that what we eat has a good deal to do with our level of health. Many teachings confirm the view that we are what we eat. The connection has to be made and diet will undoubtedly come into the picture at some point or other. However, I feel that in all our minds it should be a HEALTH and Diet link. Not only that, but also that this way of eating can be a most pleasurable experience. How much better still, if we were to teach our children a health promoting way of eating, by introducing them to natural wholefoods right from the start. That way, future adults would have to jump at least one hurdle less. This book could certainly help a long way towards this aim.

A good natural diet needs to consist partly of raw and partly of cooked foods. Whenever possible, ingredients should be whole and natural, not refined or prepared in any way. Vegetables and fruit should be fresh, not tinned, preserved or frozen. Organically produced food would be ideal. Buy as few as possible of the manufactured and commercially prepared foods. Today, perhaps more than ever, we are learning from experience that to create and maintain good health, a high level of nutrition is required. This quality of nutrition can only be found in whole natural foods. *The Bristol Recipe Book* has been produced to make the experience of preparing such foods available to everyone.

Sadhya, and everyone who has contributed to this book, is showing you that healthy eating can certainly be enjoyable, maybe even more enjoyable than the way you are eating now. She has compiled recipes which show that this way of eating can be as attractive, as tasty and as delicious as any way of eating can be. Please open your heart and your senses to the pleasures of eating real food. Try it!

Ute Brookman
Diet-Therapist
Bristol Cancer Help Centre.

Introduction

The diet which has evolved over the past three or so years at the Cancer Help Centre is based on our experience and also the experiences of you, the patients.

The original diet as devised by Dr Alec Forbes was very strict and we were perhaps rather zealous in our presentation of it. Some patients unfortunately became over-anxious and even obsessed with what was 'good' and what was 'bad' food, to the point where they weren't enjoying what they ate. We used to have a four star system for grading all ingredients. It has become obvious that nothing is as simple as this. All patients are individuals with different conditions and therefore differing needs. To give a simple example, to restrict potatoes (one star) to once-a-week inclusion may be a good idea for some patients, while for others there is no reason at all why they should not eat them more frequently. It is very important to follow a dietary therapy such as ours with the advice of a doctor who knows your condition and who understands our approach in regard to diet. If at all possible visit us here at the Cancer Help Centre in Bristol to discuss your personal needs with our doctors and diet therapist.

The recipes given in this book are based on the meals we serve every day to our resident patients and to day-visiting patients (and to our staff). For some patients we may do special dishes to meet their particular requirements.

The diet recommended in this book will be found to be extremely good for all your family. It is a well balanced vegan diet (with one or two small additions mentioned later).

We believe you will notice an improvement in your health and vitality within a few weeks and that you will choose to continue to eat in this way long after you have regained your health.

How to Approach the Diet

We usually recommend that this diet is moved into slowly, over a few weeks, depending on the sort of food you have eaten previously. If you have been a 'meat and two veg' person or have eaten a lot of processed or convenience food, then take a while to change over. If it is a big change treat yourself gently and allow the occasional slip. As long as you are definitely moving forward a slip will do no harm.

Give yourself a target. Say to yourself, 'In one (or two or three weeks) I will have totally changed over to my new diet.' This diet is now eaten by thousands of people. They all had to make a start. Many enjoyed the challenge of taking up something new, and the achievement of feeling so much better simply by their own actions. Some people find the change more easy than others. The main ingredient for success seems to be to not dwell on the things you can no longer eat, but to look to each meal as a new experience and to enjoy the novelty of new foods and new tastes, while learning more about food and the way it affects us so profoundly.

After you have been following this diet for a few months it will be time for a reassessment. This again should be with a doctor or diet therapist. If you are still craving animal foods or if you have lost a little weight it may be suggested that you eat an occasional piece of fish, chicken or egg. Some people's bodies do need animal protein. But if you are enjoying this food, feeling better and looking better and having more energy (and we believe you will be) then you will probably decide to stay on this diet. In fact it will no longer be a diet; it will just be the food you choose to eat because you like it and know it to be so good for you.

All the recipes in this book will serve about four people. When a teaspoon or tablespoon is mentioned the reader should use a rounded teaspoon- or tablespoonful.

What Our Diet Consists of

The easiest way to show this is in chart form and then you can cross-refer to see with what we replace an eliminated item.

WHAT WE DO USE	WHAT WE DO NOT USE
Fresh vegetables, organically grown whenever possible	Frozen or tinned vegetables
Whole grains (rice, wheat, barley, rye, maize, oats, buckwheat)	Meat, fish, eggs (at least initially – they may be reintroduced after a while)
Pulses	
Soya milk	Milk
Tofu	Cheese
Live goat's milk yoghurt	Commercial sweetened 'dead' yoghurt
Spring water	Tea, coffee, cocoa, drinking chocolate, squash, fizzy drinks
Herb tea	
Fresh fruit and vegetable juices	
Herbs and spices	Salt
Cider vinegar	Malt vinegar
Fresh and sun-dried fruit	Tinned and frozen fruit
	Commercially produced desserts
	Ice cream
100% wholemeal bread	White, shop-bought bread
Home-baked cakes and biscuits	Shop bought cakes and biscuits
Pure fruit spreads (sugar free)	Jams and marmalade
Home-made nut butter	Peanut butter
Tahini (sesame seed spread)	
Ghee	Butter, margarine, lard
Cold pressed sunflower oil	Cooking oil
Honey, malt extract	Sugar

Non-vegan Ingredients

There are just two ingredients that are animal products which we include on this diet.

Ghee   We use ghee (clarified butter) as cooking fat. This is because at cooking temperature ghee does not produce carcinogens which vegetable oils do.

Goat's milk yoghurt   We include this because it is well known that yoghurt is very helpful to the digestion, particularly for patients who have undergone chemotherapy and radio-therapy. It helps to re-establish the flora in the gut which have been wiped out by these two processes.

1

Making A Start

You're soon going to go shopping for all the new items for your store cupboard – the non perishable foods.

You need to find a wholefood shop. These shops have opened up in even the smallest towns in the past few years. They often have 'country' sounding names like Harvest, Crab Apple, Stoneground. If you have always shopped in supermarkets and grocers then you are in for a surprise. You won't usually find bright (and costly) packaging enticing you to buy something you don't want or need – just simple bags of produce, probably bagged up right there on the premises and with a simple label to inform you of the contents. Your shop will have a range of pulses, grains, nuts and seeds as well as herbs, spices, oils and vinegars, and lots more as well.

Most people who work in wholefood shops are very interested in our sort of food. Talk to them about your need for organically grown food and untreated dried fruits. They may well make special orders for you. We have to persuade the shopkeeper and ultimately the grower that the need is there.

I have compiled a starter list for you to take on your first shopping trip. As you become more familiar with the diet you will be able to extend the range.

You may be able to persuade your shop to stock 'Ecover' washing up liquid. We find this excellent. If you have trouble finding it, here is the address of the importers who should give you the address of your nearest stockist:

Ecover Importers
Full Moon
Charlton Court Farm

Mouse Lane
Steyning
West Sussex BN4 3DF

YOUR NEW KITCHEN

No, I'm not suggesting that you need to buy new storage units
or change your cooker or sink! What I do suggest is that you
take a good look at your kitchen and re-think it in terms of the
new food you will be storing and cooking.

Non perishable food

On your new diet, you will be able to stock up at your local
wholefood store once a week or even once a month. You will
need storage containers that will store this sort of food
properly. Dried food needs to be kept in airtight containers to
keep it dry; at Grove House, we find the best solution to this is
to use large sweet jars. It's possible to buy these from a local
sweet shop for about 50 pence each. In these you can actually
see how much of an ingredient you have in stock, and you'll
have a visual reminder of the variety of ingredients you can use
to give you inspiration for each meal. When filled with the
different coloured and shaped beans and grains they actually
look very attractive and will arouse lots of interest from your
friends if you have them displayed on a shelf in your kitchen.

Herbs and spices
You will find it essential to keep a variety of herbs and spices
and these can be kept in 1lb (450g) jam jars. You will find it
economical to buy herbs and spices by the ounce from your
whole food shop. Eventually you may like to grow your own
herbs and dry them, to store in your storage jars for use in the
winter.

Nuts

The best way to store nuts is to keep them in airtight containers in the fridge. Don't buy very large amounts of nuts at one time. You need to use them really fresh, as the oils in nuts soon go rancid.

Flour

All flours should be kept in airtight containers to preserve their freshness.

Perishable foods

Vegetables

You will be buying fresh vegetables every three or four days. The bottom of the fridge is a good place for your salad stuff. Always remove it from any plastic wrapping so that it can breathe. Vegetable racks are best for root vegetables, but keep potatoes in a dark place otherwise they will go green and maybe also start to sprout. Members of the brassica (cabbage) family can go into the vegetable rack if you have little room in the fridge.

Fruit

Fruit can have its own rack in a cool, airy place, but soft fruits are best kept in the fridge to prevent them overripening too quickly. Keep a bowl of washed fruit on the kitchen or dining room table so that you can help yourself to a quick snack – it always looks beautiful, too.

Bean sprouts

Don't forget to keep a space on your kitchen windowledge for a number of jars of bean sprouts or the commercial sprouter.

Starter List

BEANS
Haricot
Blackeye
Mung
Aduki
Soya (if you are going to
    make soya milk or tofu)
NUTS
Cashew
Hazel
Almonds (whole)
Chestnuts (dried)
GRAINS (all whole grain)
Rice
Millet
Buckwheat (untoasted)
Wheat
Barley (pot not pearl)
Rye
PASTA
Wholewheat spaghetti
Wholewheat macaroni
Buckwheat spaghetti
OIL
Cold pressed, unrefined
    sunflower oil
VINEGAR
Cider vinegar
HERBS AND SPICES
Basil, dill, fennel, thyme,
    sage, tarragon, marjoram,
    cumin, coriander

PEAS AND LENTILS
Chickpeas
Split peas (yellow or green)
Lentils (brown and green)
SEEDS
Sunflower
Pumpkin
Alfalfa
Sesame
SOYA PRODUCTS
Tofu
Soya milk (no sugar or salt)
FRUIT (check that all dried
    fruits have been sun dried
    and contain no sulphur)
Hunza apricots
Dates
Figs
Sultanas
CEREALS
Muesli (some commercial
    muesli contains milk
    powder, which you should
    avoid)
oats (jumbo)
SPREADS
Tahini
Nut butter (salt free)
SWEETENERS
Honey
Barley malt extract
Molasses

FLOUR
100 per cent wholewheat
organic flour (never self
raising)
TEA
Herb teas (peppermint,
rosehip, etc.)

Equipment

Refrigerator
As well as for storing some of your fresh fruits and vegetables, your fridge should be used for keeping cartons of soya milk, goat's milk yoghurt, bottles of apple juice, sunflower oil, tofu and ghee.

Food processor
If you are changing over to this diet from an 'instant' food diet you are certainly going to find the preparation more time consuming, and even from an 'ordinary British diet' you will find, at least initially, that you are spending a little more time in the kitchen than you used to. To make things easier for you, especially if you are not feeling very well at times, I suggest that you invest in a food processor. These really are wonderful machines. For many years I resisted them, thinking that I preferred to do everything in the old way, then I was persuaded to try one. Instantly I was converted. They are such fun! They are so easy to use and they save such a lot of time. If you use them in a logical order then you only have to wash them at the end of each process and usually they are so well designed that this is a very simple task. Although they vary model to model, what most will do is to blend ingredients together for cake making, or blend to a smooth purée for soups, sauces and fruit desserts. Some can be used to knead dough for bread making. For salad preparation they are indispensable if you are cooking for more than one or two. A variety of blades will grate and slice, producing salads that look irresistible and are

so finely and neatly cut that it is easy for you to eat a large helping.

Blender/grinder

If you are preparing food for only one or two and you are happy to continue to cut salads by hand, then a blender with a grinder attachment is perhaps the best choice for you. The grinder part of this machine is sometimes called the coffee bean grinder or nut mill. With this you can grind nuts to make nut sauces and creams or roughly chop nuts to add as toppings to crumbles or to include in nut roasts and burgers. You may also use the grinder for producing fresh spices. The blender globe is used for making purées and creams, for smooth sauces and fruit fools and whips. It can also be used to emulsify the oil into your carrot juice.

Juicer

A juicer is another wonderful piece of equipment. It will do what no other piece of equipment will do, and that is to separate the fibre of the fruit or vegetable and the juice. (Some people expect a blender to do this but of course all a blender will do is simply blend the fruit or vegetable to a purée, not separate the juice.)

If you want to drink health-giving juices made from fresh fruits and vegetables and if you intend to take fresh carrot juice as part of your treatment, then a juicer is an indispensable piece of equipment. We find the 'Moulinex' juicer very good value for money.

Water filter

An inexpensive and very useful piece of equipment that I recommend you to buy is a water filter. It is now possible to get one in jug form. Tap water is poured into the upper part of the jug from where it passes through a replaceable filter into the lower jug. What is removed by the filter is the chlorine and traces of heavy metals such as lead, as well as organic pollutants. It does not remove the minerals and trace elements which are not only important for the taste of water but are important for health. The filtered water tastes purer and looks clearer. The filter jugs, and replacement filters, are generally available in healthfood shops. The filter should be replaced after every 60 to 100 litres, depending on your water supply. Pure water will cost you only a few pence per litre, considerably less than bottled spring water.

Steamers

You will be steaming vegetables frequently. Although a saucepan steamer is a very nice item, it is expensive in stainless steel. A very good alternative is a basket steamer. This will fold or open to fit a variety of saucepan sizes and, in stainless steel, is a very reasonable price.

Saucepans

We want you to stop using aluminium for saucepans or any other form of cookware. It's long been known that contact between acid fruit and vegetable foods and aluminium produces aluminium poison which accumulates in the body. Teflon-coated pans are also well known to be a health hazard as during use tiny flakes of the teflon lining get worn off and contaminate the food. We suggest that you change to stainless steel, expensive I know, but it will last for years. The see-through pans made of toughened glass are all right, as are 'le Creuset' pans and casseroles.

Miscellaneous equipment

You will of course need a number of good quality knives of different sizes. Ordinary steel will take a sharper edge than stainless steel but will react to acid fruit and vegetables, so I have one or two of each for different jobs. I consider a knife sharpening steel an indispensable piece of equipment.

You will need two chopping boards (or one clearly labelled FRUIT on one side and VEG on the other). There's no pleasure in eating a delicate fruit salad that tastes of onions and garlic!

I'm assuming that you already have a selection of wooden spoons and spatulas, identifiable for sweets and savouries.

You will need a range of mixing bowls, baking trays and cake and bread tins, garlic crusher and an apple corer.

Equipment that you should not use

Microwave cookers
We want you to go back to the simplest, purest ways of cooking and eating. Microwave cooking is such a new, strange way of heating food by vibrating the molecules, and no one yet knows what the long term results may be. It may of course be shown in the future that they are a harmless piece of technology, but we would rather play safe and strongly advise you not to use one.

Pressure cookers
Although the pressure cooker is a well-tried way of cooking, unlike the micro wave, we advise that you do not use one. It is a very violent way of quickly cooking food, destroying the enzymes and particularly damaging fruits and vegetables. By carefully planning ahead there should be no necessity for you to use a pressure cooker.

2
Soya Products

The soya bean is the most nutritious vegetable grown, in terms of protein. It contains about 35 per cent protein, more than any other plant or animal foodstuff. Soya protein contains all eight of the essential amino acids and is therefore complete. You will see how useful it is to include it in your diet.

Unfortunately, the soya bean is the most difficult of beans to transform into a delicious meal. Not only does it require long soaking and cooking, it actually has very little flavour and demands a lot of expertise with flavourings to make it tasty. I don't want to put you off cooking soya beans, but if you are totally new to this sort of food then I think that until you become more familiar with bean cooking, the best and easiest way to incorporate the soya bean into your diet is through the use of soya products such as tofu and soya milk.

Both soya milk and tofu can now be easily bought from wholefood shops and the quality seems to be excellent. Just one or two points to remember; make sure that your soya milk is free from added salt and sugar. Some varieties contain added vitamin B12 which may be useful. Avoid the smoked variety of tofu; the smoked flavour is an undesirable additive.

For those of you who are interested in increasing your repertoire as cooks I've included recipes for making your own soya milk and tofu. Not only does making your own save a quite considerable amount of money, it's also a very exciting and interesting process — but if your time and energy are limited, don't worry. The bought varieties are very good and perhaps you will have a go at making your own soya milk and tofu some time in the future. However, by making your own, you will also end up with a third product which is a residue of the process of making soya milk. This product is okara and it is not yet possible to buy this over the counter. It's a real bonus to add to breads, cakes and crumble mixes, not only adding texture and lightness but added protein as well.

Soya milk

Soya milk actually contains more protein and iron than cow's milk. It is low in calories and has no cholesterol. It is easy to digest and it has an alkaline effect in the body. If you make it at home it is very cheap; 1lb (450g) of soya beans will yield about 7 pints (4 litres) of soya milk.

Uses for soya milk
Although soya milk has a rather dry, beany taste this is easily masked in cooking. It is very good when mixed with blended fruit for a milk shake or in fruit sauces. It also makes extremely tasty savoury sauces, either by the roux method with wholewheat flour and ghee, or blended and heated with arrowroot and flavoured with vegetables and herbs. It reacts just like cow's milk when cooked but has the advantage of not curdling when mixed with acid fruits.

If you enjoy a warm nightcap, try hot soya milk flavoured with malt extract. You can make 'cocoa' with the addition of a little carob powder.

To make soya milk
Soak 1¼ cups (10oz/275g) soya beans in plenty of water (filtered if possible) for about 18 to 24 hours. Change the water a couple of times as the beans may start to ferment. Drain and rinse well.

Put 11 cups (4½ pints/2.5 litres) of water in a large pan and bring to the boil. Mash the beans in your food processor. In some machines this is best done by adding some water. If you need to do this, take some from the measured volume in the saucepan. Make sure the beans are mashed to a thick cream. The smoother the cream is, the greater the milk yield will be. Add this soya cream to the boiling water in the pan, stir and adjust the heat so that the mixture is just simmering. Stir occasionally and keep simmering for 30 mins.

Line a large colander or sieve with a teatowel (rinsed to remove detergents) or use a piece of muslin. Sit the colander in a large bowl so that it is suspended. Pour your soya milk mixture into the lined colander. The milk will strain through into the bowl below. You are left with the soya fibre, okara, in the colander. You should cool the soya milk quickly and this is best done by sitting the bowl of milk in a sink of cold water.

Store your milk in sterilized containers made of china or glass. Sterilize them by immersing in boiling water for a few minutes. Keep the soya milk in the fridge and use within five or six days. You may freeze it in suitable containers to keep for up to three months.

Uses for tofu

Tofu is our equivalent of cheese in that it is made from soya milk that has been curdled to form curds and whey. The whey has been discarded and the curds pressed to produce a firm piece of tofu. It's possible to buy silken tofu which is thinner and is useful for sauces but in general we use firm tofu.

Don't expect it to taste like cheese – it doesn't. In fact, it doesn't taste of very much at all. At first this may seem to its detriment, but in fact it is its virtue because you can make it taste of whatever you like by careful flavouring. It can be either savoury or sweet. Tofu has quite a rubbery texture, but when blended it becomes a thick cream. Add blended fruit and you have quickly made a lovely fruit fool or whip. Add to this extra fruit juice and you have an instant fruit sauce or a high protein drink for those moments when you need an instant snack to keep you going for a few more hours. We also serve these high protein drinks to patients who have lost weight.

Blend tofu with herbs and vegetables and you have a savoury sauce to pour over steamed vegetables or pasta. You can also cook this sauce in a flan case with steamed vegetables to make a quiche.

Cut into small cubes, tofu can be marinated in various highly flavoured liquids and it will absorb the flavour. These cubes can then be added to stir fries, tossed into salads or added to all manner of savoury dishes such as stews, roasts and bakes or floated in soups. The cubes can also be rolled in flour and sautéed in ghee to give a crispy outside, (these go very well with Chinese-style dishes).

I hope the above ideas will show you the variety and versatility of this wonderful food.

To make tofu

Start by going through exactly the same procedure as for making soya milk but using slightly different proportions – for soya milk the proportion of beans to water is approximately 1:9, while for tofu the ratio is 1:15. This is not really crucial, and of course if you have made an amount of soya milk and you want to turn some of it into tofu then you can always add a little extra water to the milk before starting the tofu process.

Using 1¼ cups (10oz/275g) to 7½ pints (4.25 litres) water, follow the recipe for making soya milk. At the point when the milk has drained through the cloth into the bowl below you now continue with the tofu recipe.

Dissolve 2 teaspoons nigari* in 1¼ cups (½ pint/300 ml) boiling water, stirring to check that it has completely dissolved.

Rinse the saucepan in which you boiled the soya mixture, and into this pour the freshly made soya milk. Return to the heat and bring almost to boiling point. Remove from the heat.

Pour in half the nigari mixture and stir well. Settle the milk by holding a spoon on the surface. Wait for a couple of minutes and then gently trickle in the rest of the nigari mixture. Stir very gently. You will see that already curds and whey have started to form as the milk separates.

Now you need to start to remove the whey. (This can be discarded, although traditionally it was used to clean the equipment.) We take a sieve, the handle of which we have bent into an upright position, at 90°. The sieve then sits in the pan of curds and whey. The whey then forms in the sieve and can be ladled out without disturbing the curd.

When most of the whey has been removed (this can take a while), line a colander or sieve with a rinsed teatowel or muslin and sit the colander in a bowl.

Ladle the curds into the lined colander and gather the excess material up to form a bag. Place a saucer on top of the bag of curds and place a weight of 2–3lb (1–1.5kg) on it. The weight will gently force the remaining whey out of the curds and it will drip through the colander into the bowl below. It will firm the tofu. After an hour or two remove the weight, carefully untie the bag and slide the piece of tofu on to a plate.

Cut it into chunks or slices and place in a bowl, covering it with filtered or spring water. Keep in the fridge, remembering to change the water daily to keep it fresh. Use within five or six days.

Okara

This is the fibre residue which is left behind in the sieve when you strain the soya milk. Keep it in a bowl in the fridge and use within two or three days.

When you are making bread, cakes or biscuits substitute about one fifth okara for the flour in the recipe. When making nut roasts, lentil burgers or bean patties you can add some okara as a substitute for either the flour or the beans or lentils given in the recipe. It is also excellent in crumble toppings, sweet or savoury. Experiment with it and I think you will discover what a real bonus it is.

Tempeh

We have recently discovered tempeh and are so delighted with it that I want to include it in this book even though we have not fully explored all its possibilities. We have managed to buy it locally although it is not in many wholefood shops yet. I think it will become more popular and more easy to obtain.

Tempeh originates in Indonesia, where it is an important ingredient of the traditional diet. It is a sort of cake of soya beans into which a culture has been introduced. As this culture matures it forms a mould (a bit like the blue mould in some cheeses) which travels through the beans, holding them together by a fine network of myceium. The appearance of tempeh can be initially a little off-putting because of the grey to black mould, but don't be put off by its appearance. The taste when cooked is incredibly delicious – a bit like mushrooms and a bit like chicken. It's very easy to digest and because it is made from soya beans it is a complete protein.

The way that we have used it is to thinly slice the cake of tempeh and to gently fry the slices in a little ghee. I know that there are lots of traditional ways to use tempeh, making pâtés and casseroles, but as yet we have not really experimented with these so I am not able to include recipes in this book. However, I can recommend a book that includes tempeh making and recipes. It is called *Making Your Own Home Proteins* by Evelyn Findlater, published by Century Hutchinson Ltd.

We have made our own tempeh a number of times and find it an exciting process. If you want to have a go then the culture, *rhizopus oligosporus*, and very clear instruction sheets are available from the following address:

Micro Audit
Wheathampstead House
Wheathampstead
St Albans
Hertfordshire

tel. 058 283 2370
Micro Audit will also supply nigari.

Soya products to avoid

Textured vegetable protein (TVP)   is on sale in many whole-food shops. It comes in a number of forms such as dried mince or dried chunks, flavoured to resemble meat. We feel that it is unacceptable because the many processes that the humble soya bean has to go through and the numerous additives for flavour and colour take it far from its original, simple form. Avoid it!

*Nigari can be obtained from:
    Paul's Brewery
    Wheathampstead House
    Wheathampstead
    St Alban's
    Herts AL4 8QY

3
Breakfast

This is a very important meal, so don't skimp it. A good breakfast will take you through to lunch time with no temptation to snack on any thing undesirable. We always serve grain for breakfast at the Cancer Help Centre. Quite often this is muesli but we also frequently eat a rice or millet dish and sometimes barley, wheat or rye. They are always served with lots of fresh fruit and a milk or nut cream or a fruit sauce. I'll give you recipes for all of these further on.

Muesli

This can consist of different grain flakes; oats, wheat, barley, or rye, with added sun-dried fruits and nuts. Try to find an organic muesli or, alternatively, make one to your own taste. You can buy the different organic flakes at your wholefood shop, along with sun-dried fruits and fresh nuts. Then mix them in the proportion you prefer. Quite a lot of people use a high proportion of oatflakes. Make sure that these are 'jumbo' oats and not instant or 'quick' oatflakes which are not so good. If you have to buy a commercially produced muesli, examine the ingredients label. You may find that, for all its claims of health and nutrition, it actually contains some hidden extras which you would prefer to avoid, such as skimmed milk or whey powder, salt, sugar, additives to preserve the fruits, and so on.

To prepare muesli
Soak your muesli overnight if you don't enjoy it too chewy;

just cover it with either spring water or apple juice. Then in the morning add a little goat's milk yoghurt or soya milk or make one of the sauces on pages 35–8. Serve with plenty of fresh fruit in season, such as apples, pears, grapes, bananas and strawberries. Doesn't that sound delicious?

Porridge

Another good traditional breakfast is porridge made from 'jumbo' oatflakes or oatmeal. Serve it with soya milk to complete the protein balance of this winter breakfast.

Rice

Any type of brown rice will do for this dish; you don't need a special pudding rice. You can, if you wish, soak the rice overnight to speed things up a bit in the morning.

Using ½ cup (3oz/75g) brown rice to 1½ (12fl oz/350ml) cups water per person, simmer the rice in the water for about ½ hour until it is almost tender. Add ½ cup (4fl oz/120ml) soya milk per person and 1 tablespoon creamed coconut, roughly chopped. Continue to cook for about 10 minutes, stirring frequently, until the rice is tender. Other things you can add during the cooking are: sultanas; cashew nuts; chopped dates; chopped figs; sliced banana; fruit in season. You can serve this dish simply as it is, or with a little goat's milk yoghurt, or with a fruit or nut sauce (see pages 35–8).

Millet

Millet is a good breakfast food. It cooks quite quickly, taking only about 20 minutes. You can treat it in the same way as rice (see above), adjusting the cooking time. Here are some other variations which work particularly well with millet:

Instead of using water, use part water, part apple or other fruit juice.

Add a little lemon juice to the water.

Towards the end of the cooking time, stir in some Hunza apricots that have been soaked overnight, stoned and then blended with the soaking juice.

To help the texture of millet add some sunflower seeds, sprouted if you wish, or add roughly chopped or ground hazelnuts or almonds.

Again, this dish can be eaten as it is or mixed with fresh or dried fruits, or served with goat's milk yoghurt or a fruit sauce (see pages 35–8).

Barley, wheat, rye

All these grains take about an hour to cook, so I do not suggest that you cook them for breakfast, but if you have some left over in the fridge from the previous day you can transform them into a breakfast dish.

Take about ¾ cup (5oz/150g) of cooked grain per person. Place in a saucepan with a little soya milk and heat thoroughly, stirring all the time. You can add fresh fruits in season or chopped or soaked dried fruit, nuts or seeds. Instead of using soya milk you can use a fruit juice as the liquid in which to heat the grain. Serve with goat's milk yoghurt, soya milk or one of the sauces (see pages 35–8). Mulberry sauce is particularly good with these grain dishes.

Cornmeal (Polenta)

Cornmeal is much neglected in Britain. It is the flour from maize (sweetcorn). It makes a delicious breakfast and its delicate flavour goes well with fruits and sweet spices.

1 cup (8fl oz/250ml) water (or
   apple juice)
1 cup (8fl oz/250ml) soya
   milk
½ cup (2oz/50g) cornmeal

1–2 teaspoons honey
½ cup (3oz/75g) raisins
1 banana
ground nutmeg/ground
   cinnamon/cardamon pods

Heat the water or juice and the soya milk. Stir in the cornmeal. Turn the heat right down (it spits) and stir with a long-handled wooden spoon. It will soon thicken. Continue until it is smooth, adding the honey, raisins, bananas and any of the spices to your taste.

Breakfast Sauces

Serve these with your breakfast grain dishes. It is best to make them fresh each day. Once you have made a few of these sauces you will see how easy it is and you will be able to make your own versions using other fruits in season, e.g. pineapple, raspberries, strawberries, fresh figs, peaches and nectarines, mango, blackcurrants, etc.

Creamy Sauce

small piece tofu
few almonds or cashew nuts,
   ground
soya milk and/or apple juice

pinch of ground cinnamon
small amount malt extract or
   honey

Blend all the ingredients together, adjusting the amount of liquid according to whether you want a thick or thin sauce.

Mulberry Sauce

Try to find these delicious dried mulberries. They originate in

Afghanistan, where they grow alongside the Hunza apricot.

handful mulberries   *lemon juice to taste*
apple juice or *spring water*

You can soak the mulberries overnight, but this is not essential. Blend all the ingredients together until smooth.

Hunza Sauce

Hunza apricots, soaked in a   *apple juice* or *spring water*
   little water overnight

Take the stones out of the apricots, and blend the fruit with the liquid, adding more if required.

Hunza Cream

Follow the recipe for Hunza sauce but add some ground nuts, e.g. cashews, almonds or hazelnuts.

Hunza and Tofu Cream

Follow the recipe for Hunza sauce, but add a small piece of tofu and blend together. To make an extra-creamy sauce, use soya milk instead of apple juice.

Banana Milk

1 banana, chopped   *juice of ½ lemon*
soya milk   *½ teaspoon honey*

Blend together until creamy.

Cream Coconut Sauce

small piece creamed coconut,   1 teaspoon malt extract
    grated
soya milk with a little spring
    water

Blend together. To make this sauce extra delicious, soak a piece of vanilla pod in the liquid overnight or use a few drops of real vanilla essence.

Saucy Dates

a few dates, soaked overnight   pinch of ground cinnamon
    in spring water
grated rind and juice of 1
    orange

Simmer the dates in the soaking water until soft with the grated orange rind. Add the orange juice and cinnamon and blend or mash together.

Orange Sauce

2–3 oranges   a few cashew nuts or
soya milk   almonds, ground

Grate the rind of 1 orange. Put it in the blender with the pulp from all the oranges, the milk and the ground nuts. Blend.
    Variations: Try this sauce using a lemon or a grapefruit instead of one of the oranges and adding a little honey to sweeten.

Grape Sauce

small bunch black or white
  grapes

soya milk
1 teaspoon tahini

Blend all together.

Stewed Apple

2–3 apples, chopped and
  cored
grated rind and juice of 1
  orange

1 clove (optional)
a little apple juice or spring
  water

Simmer all together until the apple is fairly soft. Remove the clove, if using. Variations can be made in exactly the same way as stewed apple, such as pear.

To add extra flavour, add some sultanas, chopped figs, dates, or sliced bananas to the fruit and cook it all together.

4

Salads

The best food that you can eat to regain your health and maintain it is raw vegetables. They will give you more vitamins and minerals than any other food; they will help to remove toxins from the body and strengthen the immune system; and they will give you increased vitality and you will feel and look better.

We would like you initially to eat 75 per cent of your daily intake of food as raw vegetables and fruits. This can seem like an awful lot to start with, but give it a try and after a few weeks I think you will be surprised. Once you have become used to actually having to chew that amount (it will take longer than your old-style food), and as your digestion gets used to having lots of raw food to work on, I think you will always want to eat this way. The flavours and textures and the simple freshness will become a delight and you will find combining the different vegetables available a very creative way of preparing food.

Buy the very best quality vegetables, organically grown whenever possible. It's becoming easier by the week to buy organic food. Even just a year ago we were having to buy quite a lot of non-organic vegetables and fruit for the kitchen at the Cancer Help Centre. Now 99 per cent is organic. Some weeks the only non-organic thing I buy is bananas, which continue to be a problem.

In Bristol in the last twelve months, six greengrocers have 'gone organic'. This has happened by the public creating the demand, and by suppliers filling it. This can happen in your town too. I've also been delighted to note that sometimes the price of organically grown produce has actually been cheaper than its non-organic equivalent. Things are definitely looking up. In some areas, though it is not so easy and it is often impossible to travel to a greengrocer's on the other side of town as often as you would like. Try an advertisement in the classified section of your local newspaper, 'Cancer patient on special diet needs to buy supplies of organically grown produce. Can any gardener or allotment holder please help'. People who garden organically are people who care. They are often delighted to sell their produce to those who really appreciate it. Those of you who are gardeners will know that gardens very often produce gluts and there are far more runner beans or cabbages at that time than one family can consume.

At those times when it is not possible to buy organic vegetables, don't panic! Just buy the best, freshest vegetables possible. Wash them in a solution of 2 tablespoons of malt vinegar to a washing up bowl of water. For very delicate flavoured things such as soft fruits you can use cider vinegar instead. This will remove any traces of chemical spray. It won't of course change what is inside the produce as the result of being fed chemical fertilizers.

As soon as vegetables are harvested, they start to deteriorate, only 30 minutes after a lettuce has come out of the ground it has lost 40 per cent of its vitamin C, so it is very important to use really fresh vegetables and fruits. Prepare your salad immediately before each meal. If it has to stand for even a short time, cover it with a plate. A salad that has been standing for a few hours will be little more than vegetable fibre. One of the ingredients in a fresh vegetable, along with the nutrients, is something that cannot be weighed or measured but definitely exists and is vitally important to you. That ingredient is life. This is one of the reasons why we stress the importance of growing and eating bean sprouts. As you put them into your mouth and eat them they are still alive. They are one of the best foods that you can eat.

Bean sprouts

By growing your own bean sprouts you are providing yourself
and your family with one of the best foods available. I'm using
the term bean sprouts, but of course I'm including grain
sprouts and seed sprouts as well.

We know that in their dried form beans, grains and seeds are
an excellent protein food. When we sprout them there is a huge
increase in the quantity of vitamins and amino acids. The
vitamins vary bean to bean, seed to seed, grain to grain. Some
contain vitamin C, some B complex vitamins, and some
vitamin A. So you will see that it is good to grow a variety of
sprouts not only for their varying tastes and textures but also
for the nutritional value.

There are a number of different ways to grow bean sprouts,
but they all follow the same principle in that they are soaked
for a number of hours, drained and then rinsed two or three
times daily to keep them moist and fresh. The sprouts will be
ready to eat in between three and five days depending on
variety and also time of year; in spring and summer all sprouts
will grow a little quicker.

In the Cancer Help Centre kitchen we grow our bean
sprouts in large glass sweet jars. This gives a lot of sprouts.
You won't be feeding so many people (I presume!) so you can
use 8 oz (225g) clear glass coffeejars, or a bean sprouter. These
are easy to obtain from kitchen shops. They usually have three
tiers so you can grow three different types of sprout at the same
time. Some people suggest that you grow your sprouts in the
dark, in the airing cupboard, or under the sink. We don't find
this is necessary; in fact, we prefer to keep them where we can
see them to remind us to rinse them frequently. They seem very
tolerant of a wide extreme of temperature, anywhere between
50°F and 70°F (10°C and 21°C), but we do find that we need to
protect them from midday sunshine in the middle of summer
by covering them with a damp teatowel. The main thing to
remember is that the warmer they are, the more frequently

they will need rinsing to keep them cool and sweet.

You will find that your family and friends are very interested in your 'indoor gardening' and you will derive a great deal of satisfaction from growing your own food and knowing that it is fresh, pure and very good for you. You may find that you have green fingers with some sprouts and not with others. This may be due to the quality of the seed that you are using. Another thing to remember is that only whole beans will grow; a bean that has been hulled and split in half no longer has the potential to grow, so split red lentils or yellow or green split peas are no good for sprouting.

Try three or four different sprouts to start with and when you have the hang of it, increase your repertoire. It's a good idea to start a different sprout each day so that you don't have too many ready at the same time, although if you have a glut, you can always put the sprouts in polythene bags in the fridge and use them within a day or two.

It's useful to buy a sieve which just fits over the neck of your sprouting jars, then you simply fill the jar with water, place the sieve on the jar and invert the whole thing.

Procedure
Take 2 small handfuls of your chosen bean (this will yield about 8oz (225g) of sprouts). Check for grit and dirt and rinse in a sieve under running water.

Place in your 8oz (225g) jar and add plenty of cold water. I suggest you use filtered or spring water for this soaking stage as the beans are going to absorb a lot of water and with it fluoride and other chemical nasties if you use tap water. Soak for about 12 hours, except in the case of soya beans which should be soaked for about 18 hours, changing the water once or twice.

Drain through your sieve, fill up with cold tap water, drain again and place the jar on its side in a convenient place, ideally on the window ledge by the sink. Top up the jar with cold tap water two or three times a day, put the sieve over the neck of the jar, invert and allow all the water to drain away. It's important not to leave a puddle of water sitting in the jar as it will soon become smelly.

Check the following chart for growing times (between two and five days). When your sprouts have reached the desired length, rinse one more time and add to your salads.

SPROUTING CHART

VARIETY	LENGTH OF SPROUT	NO. OF DAYS
Alfalfa seeds	1 in (2.5 cm)	4/5
Sunflower seeds	¼ in (5 mm)	2/3
Fenugreek seeds	½ in (1 cm)	3/4
Aduki beans	½ in (1 cm)	4/5
Chick peas*	½ in (1 cm)	4/5
Brown lentils	¼–½ in (5 mm–1 cm)	4/5
Mung beans	½–1 in (1–2.5 cm)	4/5
Soya beans*	½ in (1 cm)	4/5
Wheat grains	¼–½ in (5 mm–1 cm)	3/5
Rye grains	¼–½ in (5 mm–1 cm)	3/5
Cannellini beans*	½ in (1 cm)	4/5
Haricot beans*	½ in (1 cm)	4/5

One more thing to mention; beans contain substances which make them difficult to digest sometimes, and they cause flatulence. To make them easy to digest I recommend that you follow this procedure: The larger beans, marked * (and any other large beans that you have sprouted) should be picked through, discarding any that have failed to sprout. Place the bean sprouts in a steamer and steam for 8 minutes, except in the case of soya beans, which should be steamed for about 12 minutes.

It is because of this problem of flatulence that I never suggest that kidney beans are sprouted. Of course all the other bean, seed, and grain sprouts should be eaten raw.

As well as adding the bean and seed sprouts to your salads you can also make a delicious pâté or dip with them. Here are some recipes to try.

Alfalfa Sprout Pâté

handful alfalfa sprouts
2 teaspoons tahini
squeeze of lemon juice

1 tablespoon chives or spring
onions (chopped)

Blend until creamy, adding water and more lemon juice for consistency and flavour.

Lentil Sprout Pâté

handful brown or green lentil
sprouts
a little sunflower oil
a little cider vinegar

black pepper
paprika
pinch of dried tarragon

Blend and adjust the seasonings.

Quick Hummus

small cube of tofu
handful of steamed chickpea
sprouts (or haricot beans)
1 clove garlic

lemon juice
black pepper
a little sunflower oil

Blend until creamy. You can add more garlic and lemon juice to taste.

Sunflower shoots

If you are enjoying sprouting your beans, perhaps you would like to take this indoor gardening one step further and grow your own sunflower shoots. These are actually grown in soil and are harvested when they are about 3 in (7.5 cm) tall. They can be added to your salads, and incredibly delicious and nutritious they are too. You need unhulled sunflower seeds for this process. Although you can use the sunflower seeds that pet shops sell as bird seed, I recommend that you buy organic seed from an organic seedsman such as Chase, who will supply you by post. The address is:

Chase Compost Grown Seeds,
Benhall,
Saxmundham,
Suffolk.

Procedure
Take a handful of sunflower seeds and soak overnight in plenty of cold tap water. Drain. Line a seed tray with 1½ in (4 cm) soil (organic if possible), and water it. Sprinkle the seeds evenly over the top of the soil. Soak 3 layers of newspaper in water and then cover the seed tray with this. Leave for 3–4 days, keeping the newspaper wet by spraying.

Check that the seed has germinated and put down shoots. If so, remove the newspaper and move the tray to a well-lit window ledge, or the conservatory or greenhouse if you are lucky enough to have one. Keep the soil moist by gentle watering or spraying.

The shoots are ready to harvest in 7–10 days when they have 2 leaves (coteledons) which have dropped the original seed case. Harvest by cutting with scissors at the base of the stem. Rinse in a colander or sieve and add to salads. You will need to use fresh soil each time you grow your shoots. Sunflower shoots do not grow successfully during winter.

Salad recipes

I've listed these salad recipes by the season, but you will find that naturally many of them overlap. Also, because so many vegetables are imported, we are no longer governed in our eating by the seasons; tomatoes, lettuces, cucumbers, radishes, watercress and most other salad items are available throughout the year (but the price will be higher). It is best to eat the vegetables in season and locally grown whenever possible. For instance, in February choose purple sprouting broccoli that has been picked locally in preference to hothouse grown lettuce from Holland. Of course it's fine to include some imported produce to make your salads more interesting and ring the changes.

I have not given proportions or amounts in the following salad recipes. You will be able to judge how much is a serving for yourself and your family. Just prepare enough for one meal, but make sure that it's plenty!

Everything in these recipes can be changed according to what is available. Don't put a recipe aside because it calls for (for example) alfalfa sprouts and white cabbage, and you have Chinese leaves in your vegetable rack and sprouted mung beans in your bean sprouter. Use these and give your salad a new name!

Of course, you can use different dressings too. If your favourite uses lemon juice rather than cider vinegar, then go ahead and make it with lemon juice. These recipes are simply to give you some idea of the variety of salads available, to stimulate your imagination (and your taste buds); they are by no means rules that must be strictly followed.

One very important thing to remember when preparing root vegetables for salads or for cooking is to leave the skins on. We peel very little and then only because the skin is very tough, as in celeriac, kohl rabi, or swede. For all other roots, including potatoes, carrots, beetroot and turnip, simply scrub under running water, cutting any damaged parts away. Most of the goodness in roots is found just below and in the skin. For those tough-skinned vegetables I have mentioned, save any parings to put into your vegetable stock, as in this way you will still be getting some of the goodness from them.

SPRING SALADS

March Winds Salad

purple sprouting broccoli, finely chopped
iceberg lettuce, finely shredded

radishes, whole or sliced
cucumber, cut into fine sticks
alfalfa sprouts

Dressing: avocado, cider vinegar, sunflower oil, black pepper. Blend all together to a thin cream consistency.

Eat All The Salad Salad

watercress, stalks chopped and leaves separated
mange tout, sliced

iceberg lettuce, finely shredded
tomato, sliced
mung bean sprouts

Dressing: sunflower oil, lemon, cider vinegar, thyme, chopped chives, mustard seeds, black pepper. Whisk all together.

Red Salad

The cauliflower will turn pink!

beetroot, grated
carrot, grated
celeriac, grated
aduki bean sprouts

cauliflower, cut into small florets
sunflower seed sprouts

Dressing: lemon juice, orange or grapefruit juice, sunflower oil, grated fresh ginger. Whisk all together.

Oriental Salad

This one is very spicy.

iceberg lettuce, finely shredded
fennel bulb, finely sliced
carrot, chopped or *grated*

courgette, cut into fine sticks
fenugreek seeds, sprouted
red kidney beans, cooked and marinated in lemon juice

Dressing: sunflower oil, lemon juice.

Japanese Salad

courgettes, cut into fine sticks
cucumber, finely diced
chicory leaves, finely shredded

watercress, broken into small sprigs
sunflower seeds
pumpkin seeds, toasted

Dressing: watercress stalks, tahini, lemon juice, black pepper, dill tops. Blend all together.

Surprising Almond Salad

watercress, torn into small sprigs, stalks chopped
apple, diced

mung bean sprouts
carrot, grated
almonds, toasted

Dressing: lemon juice, apple juice, cinnamon, black pepper. Whisk all together.

Alfred the Salad

cauliflower, finely chopped
tomato, finely chopped
chicory heart, finely chopped

lettuce, finely chopped
mange tout, finely chopped
alfalfa sprouts

Dressing: tomato, ground cashew nuts, cider vinegar, sunflower oil, black pepper. Blend all together.

Colourful Salad

cauliflower, cut into small
  florets
orange, segmented
Chinese leaves, finely
  chopped or torn

celery, finely sliced, leaves
  chopped small
cress
brown lentil sprouts

Dressing: sunflower oil, lemon juice, small amount of honey, crushed garlic clove. Blend all together.

Grove House Salad

chick pea sprouts, steamed
  for 10 minutes
calabrese, finely chopped
Chinese leaves, shredded

bobby beans, sliced into 1 in
  (2.5 cm) pieces and lightly
  steamed

Dressing: spring onions, apple juice, lemon juice, sunflower oil, alfalfa sprouts, tahini. Blend together. Add the warm, steamed chick pea sprouts and leave for 20 minutes before adding the salad ingredients.

Kidney Bean Salad

mushrooms, sliced
kidney beans, cooked
courgettes, sliced into fine
  rings

white cabbage, finely sliced
watercress broken into small
  sprigs of leaves
green lentil sprouts

Dressing: sunflower oil, cider vinegar, garlic, paprika, marjoram, black pepper. Blend together. Marinate the mushrooms and beans for 30 minutes in the dressing before adding the other ingredients.

The Grate Salad

celeriac, grated
carrot, grated

apple, grated

Dressing: sunflower oil, orange juice, cumin seeds or powder. Whisk.

Another Grate Salad

beetroot, grated
carrot, grated

apple, grated
onion, finely chopped

Dressing: sunflower oil, orange juice, grated orange rind, grated fresh ginger, caraway seeds. Whisk all together.

Rabbit's Salad

spring cabbage heart,
  chopped
avocado, cut into chunks and
  dipped in lemon juice

kohl rabi, diced
mung bean sprouts
almonds, toasted

Dressing: tofu, sunflower oil, lemon juice, dill tops. Blend to a creamy consistency.

Saint David's Favourite Salad

*leeks (the white part), finely
    sliced
white cabbage, shredded*

*radishes, sliced
turnip, finely diced
wheat grain sprouts*

Dressing: sunflower oil, cider vinegar, fennel seeds, honey, ground mustard seeds, black pepper. Blend all together.

Fennel Salad

*fennel bulb, cut into fine
    strips
kohl rabi, cut into
    matchsticks
arame seaweed, rinsed,
    soaked and well drained*

*white cabbage, shredded
clementine or orange,
    segmented
aduki bean sprouts*

Dressing: tofu, soya milk, apple juice, lemon juice. Blend to a fairly thick cream.

Brown Rice Salad

*brown rice, cooked and
    allowed to cool
carrot, finely diced
apple, finely sliced or diced
mange tout, sliced in diagonal
    strips*

*leek or onion, finely chopped
cashew nuts, slightly toasted
sesame seeds, slightly toasted*

Dressing: sunflower oil, lemon juice, fresh coriander leaves (if available) or parsley, finely chopped. Whisk all together.

SUMMER SALADS

Deckchair Salad

courgettes, diagonally sliced   *garden peas*
carrot, grated   *wheat sprouts*

Dressing: apple juice, sunflower oil, lemon juice, honey, oregano. Mix well together.

A Day by the Sea Salad

spring onions, finely sliced   *radishes, sliced or quartered*
baby carrots, sliced   *lettuce leaves, torn*
   lengthways   *mung bean sprouts*
new potatoes, steamed until
   tender

Dressing: goat's milk yoghurt, chives, parsley, honey, all blended to a thin green cream.

Sunny Salad

tomatoes, sliced   *broad beans, steamed for*
watercress, broken into   *about 4 minutes until*
   sprigs, stalks chopped   *tender*
spring onion, finely chopped   *sunflower seed sprouts*

Dressing: summer savoury, chives and basil, all chopped very finely and whisked with lemon juice and sunflower oil.

Lunch on the Lawn Salad

broad beans, steamed until
   tender
cos lettuce, torn
tomatoes, chopped

courgettes (yellow or green),
   sliced
alfalfa sprouts

Dressing: sunflower oil, lemon juice, tofu, summer savoury, apple juice. Blend together.

Bean and Then It's Gone Salad

young broad beans in their
   pods, chopped and
   steamed for 8 minutes
cabbage, shredded

cucumber, diced
tomato, sliced
alfalfa sprouts

Dressing: sunflower oil, garlic or spring onions, rosemary, lemon juice. Blend all together.

Lazy Hazy Days Salad

garden peas
new potatoes, steamed and
   sliced
spinach leaves, shredded

courgettes, cut into fine sticks
crisp lettuce, torn
sesame seeds, lightly toasted

Dressing: sunflower oil, cider vinegar, finely chopped mint, black pepper. Whisk.

Munchy, Crunchy Salad

cauliflower, chopped small
courgettes, cut into sticks or
   slices
radish, cut into quarters

spring onion, finely chopped
mung bean sprouts
sunflower seeds, lightly
   toasted

Dressing: goat's milk yoghurt, tahini, lemon juice, honey, oregano. Blend to a cream.

Sweet, Sweetcorn Salad

sweetcorn cobs, steamed,
   corn cut off
potatoes, cubed, steamed
   until tender and cooled

radish, sliced
spring onions, cut into ½ in
   (1 cm) lengths
green lentil sprouts

Dressing: sunflower oil, lemon juice, sage, chopped rosemary. Whisk.

Mysterious Salad

cauliflower, cut into florets,
   green leaves and stalks
   finely sliced
tender beetroot leaves,
   shredded
tomato, chopped

red pepper, very finely diced
onion, sliced into thin rings
   and separated
mushroom, finely sliced
green lentil sprouts

Dressing: sunflower oil, lemon juice, tomato, oregano. Blend together.

Fruity Salad

lettuce, finely shredded
courgettes, cut into
    matchsticks
peach, diced

tomato, diced
cress
grapes, halved
alfalfa sprouts

Dressing: sunflower oil, lemon juice, chopped lemon balm, thyme, all whisked together.

Sweet and Sour Salad

cos lettuce, finely shredded
avocado pear, cut into
    chunks and dipped in
    lemon juice

green grapes, halved
alfalfa sprouts
sesame seeds, lightly roasted

Dressing: sunflower oil, lemon juice, chives, black pepper. Whisk together.

Haymaker's Salad

green cabbage heart,
    shredded
garden peas
cucumber, sliced
tomato, sliced

almonds, lightly toasted
alfalfa sprouts
tofu, cut into small cubes

Dressing: sunflower oil, cider vinegar, mint, summer savoury. Whisk together.

Last Day of the Holiday Salad

French or *runner beans,*
snapped and steamed for 4
minutes
courgettes, cut into thin sticks

garden peas
carrot, diced
sweet corn cobs, steamed for
10 minutes, corn cut off

Dressing: sunflower oil, cider vinegar, summer savoury, sesame seeds. Whisk all together. Sprinkle with parsley.

Quite Unusual Potato Salad

new potatoes (small),
steamed with mint
cucumber, diced

garden peas
baby turnips, grated

Dressing: goat's milk yoghurt. Mix into the salad and sprinkle with marigold petals.

Steamed Baby Beetroot in Creamy Sauce

baby beetroot, steamed either
whole or *in chunks*

lentil sprouts

Dressing: goat's milk yoghurt, grated orange rind and juice, tofu, chopped tarragon. Blend all together and stir into the beetroot while it is still warm. Top with the lentil sprouts.

Eat It All Salad

mange tout, sliced or snapped
spinach or *turnip leaves,*
shredded

carrots, cut into long sticks
radishes, cut into quarters
mung bean sprouts

Dressing: sunflower oil, lemon juice, spring onion or garlic.
Blend well.

AUTUMN SALADS
Peking Salad

*watercress, broken into
  sprigs
satsumas, peeled and sliced
  into rings*

*Chinese leaves, finely sliced
Swiss chard leaves and stalks,
  finely chopped
green lentil sprouts*

Dressing: orange juice, sunflower oil, ground cinnamon, black
pepper. Mix all together.

Red Sky at Night Salad

*beetroot, grated
celeriac, grated
Japanese radish (diakon),
  grated*

*turnip, grated
sesame seeds, toasted*

Dressing: sunflower oil, cider vinegar, dill tops, grated ginger.
Whisk all together.

Crudités

*carrot, cut lengthways into
  long sticks
courgette, cut lengthways
  into long sticks*

*celery, cut into sticks
peppers (red and green), cut
  into long strips*

Dip: tofu, avocado, garlic, lemon juice, cider vinegar, black
pepper, parsley, all blended together. Place the bowl of dip in

the centre of a large plate and arrange the sticks of vegetables around it.

Colouring Book Salad

chick pea sprouts, steamed
    until tender (10 minutes)
calabrese, cut into small
    pieces
sweetcorn cob, steamed until
    tender, corn cut off

apple, diced and dipped in
    lemon juice
red pepper, cut into thin
    slivers

Dressing: lemon juice, sunflower oil, honey. Whisk and put the hot steamed chick pea sprouts in and when cool add the other salad ingredients.

At the Savoy Salad

calabrese or cauliflower,
    sliced (in food processor if
    possible)
mushrooms, thinly sliced
courgettes, cut into
    matchsticks

apple (red skinned), sliced
    and dipped in lemon juice
red and green lentil sprouts
parsley, chopped

Dressing: sunflower oil, apple juice, lemon juice, caraway seeds, garlic. Squeeze the garlic, whisk with the other ingredients.

Falling Leaves Salad

cabbage, shredded
Chinese radish, grated
arame seaweed, soaked and
    drained

cashew nuts, lightly toasted
mung bean sprouts

Dressing: sunflower oil, cider vinegar, grated fresh ginger, black pepper, dill seeds. Whisk.

First Frost Salad

iceberg lettuce, shredded
green grapes, whole or *halved*
pear, cut into thin slices and
   dipped in lemon juice

green pepper, finely diced
radishes, sliced
alfalfa sprouts

Dressing: goat's milk yoghurt, ground white mustard seed, dill tops. Mix all together, stir in the salad and sprinkle with paprika.

The Original Red Salad

Beetroot, grated
carrot, grated
apple, grated

kohl rabi, grated
wheat grain sprouts

Dressing: sunflower oil, apple juice, toasted cumin seeds, honey. Blend together.

Ploughperson's Salad

beetroot, diced, steamed for
   10 minutes and cooled
pear, cut into chunks and
   dipped in lemon juice

onion, cut into thin rings
mung bean sprouts

Dressing: lemon juice, marjoram, thyme. Whisk together.

Harvest Home Salad

potatoes (waxy if possible),
  diced and steamed until
  tender
celery, cut into ½ in (1 cm)
  pieces, leaves chopped
apple (russet), sliced and
  dipped in lemon juice

sultanas, soaked in apple
  juice until plump
onion, finely chopped
soya bean sprouts, steamed
  for 15 minutes until tender

Dressing: tofu, lemon juice, mint, apple juice, celery seed, ground white mustard seed. Blend and thin to a mayonnaise consistency.

Salad of Many Colours

sweetcorn cob, steamed, corn
  cut off and cooled
black grapes, halved
tomato, cut into eighths
kohl rabi, diced

cress
watercress, broken into
  sprigs
brown lentil sprouts

Dressing: sunflower oil, apple or grape juice, honey. Whisk.

Dream of Portugal Salad

mushrooms, sliced
courgette, diced
red pepper, cut into long, fine
  strips

cabbage, finely chopped
aduki bean sprouts

Dressing: sunflower or, if available, olive oil, lemon juice, garlic, grated fresh ginger, a little honey. Whisk together, pour over the mushrooms, and leave to marinate for 30 minutes.

Add the other ingredients and sprinkle with paprika and roughly chopped hazelnuts.

Shorter Days Salad

pears, sliced and dipped in
  lemon juice
cauliflower, grated

Chinese radish (daikon),
  grated
carrot, cut into matchsticks
parsley, chopped

Dressing: goat's milk yoghurt, lemon juice, chopped onion, ground white mustard seeds. Blend together. This dressing should be creamy.

September Salad

calabrese, finely chopped
tomato, sliced
mushrooms, sliced
onion, cut into fine rings

lettuce, torn
alfalfa sprouts
pumpkin seeds, toasted

Dressing: sunflower oil, cider vinegar, tomato, basil, marjoram, black pepper, garlic. Blend all together.

Tropical Beetroot Salad

beetroot, grated
pineapple, chopped into
  cubes, juice reserved

onion or spring onion,
  chopped
rye grain sprouts

Dressing: sunflower oil, pineapple juice, garlic. Squeeze the garlic and whisk all together. Decorate with watercress or parsley.

Nearly a Waldorf Salad

*apples (russets if possible),
    sliced and dipped in lemon
    juice
banana, sliced and dipped in
    lemon juice
celery, cut into ½ in (1 cm)
    pieces*

*spring onion or onion,
    chopped
cress
sunflower seed sprouts
alfalfa sprouts*

Dressing: ground cashew nuts, soya milk, lemon juice, celery seeds, dill tops. Blend to a thin cream.

WINTER SALADS

Red Square Salad

*red cabbage, chopped
spring onions, chopped
orange segments*

*apple, diced
ryegrain sprouts*

Dressing: sunflower oil, cider vinegar, orange juice, parsley. Whisk together. You should use a stainless steel knife to chop the red cabbage or it will turn blue.

Sweet Potato Salad

*sweet potatoes, cubed,
    steamed until tender and
    cooled
leeks (white part), sliced*

*purple sprouting broccoli, cut
    into small pieces
sunflower seed sprouts*

Dressing: sunflower oil, lemon juice, crushed garlic, cumin seeds. Whisk all together.

Green, Green, Green

white cabbage, finely sliced
Chinese leaves, torn or
   chopped
watercress, broken into small
   sprigs

fennel, bulb finely sliced, leaf
   chopped
avocado, cut into chunks and
   dipped in lemon juice
mung bean sprouts

Dressing: watercress (the stalks will do), sunflower oil, cider
vinegar, tofu. Blend all together.

Snowy Carrot Salad

carrots, grated
onion or leek, finely chopped

raisins, soaked in a little apple
   juice until plump
desiccated coconut

Dressing: lemon juice. Combine the carrots, onion or leek
slices, lemon juice and raisins with their apple juice and
sprinkle the coconut on top.

Bulghur Wheat Salad

bulghur wheat, soaked in
   boiling water until soft,
   and cooled
leeks (white part), sliced

swede, grated
carrot, grated
lentil sprouts
mung bean sprouts

Dressing: lemon juice, black pepper, caraway seeds.

Red Sea Salad

swede, grated
beetroot, grated
carrot, grated

apple, grated
sultanas, soaked

Dressing: sunflower oil, apple juice, cumin seeds, pinch of garam masala. Whisk well.

Brussels Salad

Brussels sprouts, finely chopped
white cabbage, finely chopped

red pepper, cut into slivers
sunflower seeds, roasted
brown lentil sprouts

Dressing: small piece of leek, sunflower oil, cider vinegar, honey. Blend.

Bombay Salad Baba

chick pea sprouts, steamed for 10 minutes and put into the dressing to cool
carrots, diced

white cabbage, finely chopped
tomato, diced
brown lentil sprouts

Dressing: lemon or lime juice, sunflower oil, paprika, pinch of garam masala. Whisk all together, marinate the chick pea sprouts and when cool add the other ingredients.

The Great Soya Bean Salad

soya bean sprouts, steamed for 20 minutes until soft and cooled
onion or leek, finely chopped
watercress, broken into sprigs

calabrese or broccoli, cut into small pieces
kohl rabi, diced

Dressing: sunflower oil, cider vinegar, garlic, black pepper, apple juice. Blend together.

In the Bleak Mid Salad

red cabbage, finely sliced
onion, finely chopped
turnip, finely diced
apple, diced and dipped in
  lemon juice

parsley, broken into small
  sprigs or finely chopped
cress
green lentil sprouts

Dressing: sunflower oil, orange juice, grated fresh ginger, caraway seeds. Whisk all together.

Blake's Dream Salad

Jerusalem artichokes, sliced
  and dipped in lemon juice
watercress, broken into small
  sprigs

leeks (white part), sliced
Savoy cabbage, finely sliced
sunflower seed sprouts

Dressing: tomato, sunflower oil, cider vinegar, basil, tofu. Blend all together to a creamy consistency.

Beetroot Surprise

beetroot, sliced and steamed until tender

Marinade: cider vinegar, basil, thyme, black pepper, grated orange peel. Steep the beetroot in the liquid for about 30 minutes. Drain.

The Orange and the Green Salad

kale, very finely chopped
lettuce, torn
avocado, cut into chunks and
  dipped in lemon juice

orange, cut into small pieces
pumpkin seeds, toasted
alfalfa sprouts

Dressing: sunflower oil, orange juice, lemon juice, black pepper, dill tops. Whisk all together.

Avocado Special

avocado, halved, stoned and   grapes
*   brushed with lemon juice*

Dressing: tofu, lemon, garlic, black pepper, parsley. Blend all together to a thick cream. Pile into the avocado halves and top with grapes and a sprig of parsley.

Crunchy Salad

cauliflower, cut into small   cress
*   florets, stalk sliced   hazelnuts, toasted and*
white cabbage, finely   roughly chopped
*   chopped   green lentil sprouts*
celery, cut into thin slices

Dressing: tofu, lemon juice, tahini, spring water, celery leaves, dill tops. Blend to the consistency of thin cream.

Pink Rice Salad

brown rice, cooked and   fennel bulb, thinly sliced
*   cooled   red lentil sprouts*
beetroot, grated
apple, diced and dipped in
*   lemon juice*

Dressing: sunflower oil, cider vinegar, pinch of garam masala. Whisk all together.

5

The Cooked Dish

For lunch and supper at the Cancer Help Centre we serve a cooked dish. This usually comprises a combination of grain, pulses (peas, beans and lentils), or nuts, with the addition of vegetables and perhaps a sauce or gravy. This dish, together with a large helping of salad, provides a complete meal. It contains all the protein and carbohydrate you require. It is necessary for you to understand a little on the combining of different proteins to give you a complete protein meal. A good soup eaten with wholemeal or oat or rye bread and a salad can be eaten at one meal instead of the cooked dish if you find it fits more conveniently with your lifestyle.

Try to think of the cooked dish as complementing the salad, rather than it being the 'main dish' with the salad as the accompaniment. You can round off the meal with fruit in many different forms (see the section on desserts).

Combining Proteins

On a vegan diet such as we are suggesting it is possible to obtain first class protein comparable to eating meat or fish, but it does require a little thought until you get the hang of it. For example, if you were to eat just beans as your allocation of cooked food at one meal you would not be getting a first class protein. The beans have to be combined with another protein food. I will try to explain this in very simple terms. For those who want to study this subject in greater depth I would recommend a book called *Diet for a Small Planet* by Frances

Moore Lappe. There are three sorts of vegetable protein;
Grains: rice, millet, oats, rye, barley, maize, buckwheat, wheat.
Pulses: peas, beans, lentils (all legumes).
Nuts and seeds: hazelnuts, almonds, brazils, walnuts, cashews, pumpkin seeds, sunflower seeds, sesame seeds.

To produce a first class protein it is necessary to combine items from two groups at one meal. You can include more than one ingredient from a group, or from all the groups; the main thing is to check that two groups are represented. This is because you need to build up the complex jigsaw that makes the amino acids. In animal protein this is complete but, apart from the soya bean which is a complete vegetable protein, other vegetable proteins are short in their chemistry and need to combine with a protein in another group to complete the jigsaw picture.

This may at first sound a bit complicated, but in fact you would probably be making these combinations automatically. If you are eating a good variety of ingredients it is unlikely that you would fail to make a complete protein. Throughout the world, people on a vegetarian diet are doing it without knowing the word protein, let alone amino acids. For instance, in India the staple diet is rice and dhal. Rice is from the grain group and dhal is made from either split peas or lentils, both pulses. In Africa, maize or millet (grains) are eaten with beans (pulses). Nearer to home, baked beans on toast provides a complete protein meal; the beans are pulses and the toast is made from flour, a grain.

Now I will give you some examples from our diet and you will see how easy it is.

Example 1
You decide to cook a rice dish (for rice you could substitute any other grain, e.g. rye, barley, millet).
With the grain you could serve a lentil sauce (or split pea or bean sauce).
Or you could make a tahini sauce (sesame seed paste).

Or you could include some nuts (or seeds) with the grain.
Or add them to the accompanying vegetables.
Or add them to the salad.
Or you could serve a nut or seed cream with a fruit dessert. As long as they are eaten at the same meal the protein will be combined.

Example 2

Suppose you make a bean stew (pulses).
Eat some wholemeal bread with it, or oatcakes (the grain).
Or thicken it with some grain flour, for instance wheat, rice or soya.
Or eat your stew with a grain such as millet or buckwheat.
Or have a rice salad with it.

Example 3

You make a nut roast.
Add to the mixture some cooked split peas, or some lentils.
Or some okara if you have been making soya milk.
Or make a lentil gravy.
Alternatively, you could follow the nut roast with a fruit crumble with a topping made from oat or wheat flakes.

Beans, Peas and Lentils (the pulses)

Beans

There is a whole variety of beans which can be used to form the basis of really tasty dishes. They come in many colours, shapes and sizes and, of course, flavours. Here are some that we regularly use: aduki beans, butter beans, soya beans, haricot beans, red kidney beans, cannellini beans, butter beans. This is just a start.

There is an excellent book by Rose Elliot called *The Bean Book*, published by Fontana. If you are new to bean cooking you will find it most useful. She describes all the beans fully and gives lots of recipes, many of them traditional. You will be able to adapt these recipes to comply with this diet.

Beans and flatulence

Beans have a reputation for causing flatulence. This is because they contain, to a greater or lesser extent depending on the variety, substances called glycosides, saponides and alkaloids. If beans are not properly cooked, these substances have a toxic effect on the digestive system, the result of which is flatulence. To cook beans correctly:

1   Pick through your measured amount of beans to remove grit, etc. Rinse.

2   Soak in three times their amount of water. It is best to use filtered water, as they are going to absorb a lot and this could mean a heavy dose of undesirable chemicals from household water. Soak overnight (for soya beans see below).

3   Drain away the soaking water and rinse. Place the beans in a saucepan with plenty of fresh water (tap water is all right for this stage).

4   Bring to the boil and maintain for 10 minutes.

5   Drain away this water and rinse again.

6   The beans are now ready for their regular cooking using either fresh water or, better still, vegetable stock. For the length of time to cook each particular bean see the following cooking chart.

Soya bean preparation

Soya beans are very tough and need to be treated slightly differently from the other beans.

Soak for between 20 and 24 hours, changing the soak water a couple of times to prevent it from going sour. You can then follow from step 3 above. A good way to speed up the cooking time is as follows; after the soaking, drain the soya beans and rinse, then place the beans in freezer bags and freeze for up to three months. When soya beans are required for cooking you can remove them from the freezer, place them in a saucepan of boiling water and when thawed proceed as from step 4 in the instructions above. You will see that in the bean cooking chart that follows I have given two different times for cooking soya beans. If they have been frozen after soaking they will cook considerably quicker.

Peas and lentils

Into this category come chick peas (garbanzos), dried green peas, split yellow and green peas, red, brown, continental and green lentils. The chick peas and whole dried peas should be treated in the same way as the beans above with a long soaking and the boiling and draining method to make them more digestible. Split peas and lentils are easier to digest and cook much more quickly, so do not require soaking.

Split peas and split red lentils are a concession to convenience foods. They are not a complete pulse as they have had their outer hull removed. However, as they cook relatively fast we feel they have their place in this diet – but do remember that they are not as nutritionally good as whole peas and lentils.

To cook peas and lentils (other than those mentioned above), pick through them to remove any grit, stones, or twigs, rinse well, and add water or vegetable stock. Simmer until soft. They will absorb about two to three times their volume of water, and take about 40 minutes to soften. Keep an eye on them for the last part of the cooking time as they may burn if they run out of liquid. They make a lovely purée with the addition of vegetables, spices and herbs, which can be served with a grain. Lentils also make an excellent quick soup.

Cooking chart

Following the soaking, rinsing, boiling, rinsing method given above, here are the approximate cooking times for beans that have been soaked overnight or, in the case of soya beans, for 20–24 hours.

Aduki beans	40 minutes
Black eyed beans	1 hour
Butter beans	1¼ hours
Cannellini beans	1¼ hours
Chick peas	1½ hours
Haricot beans	1¼ hours
Kidney beans	1½ hours
Soya beans	3–4 hours
Soya beans (soaked and frozen)	2–3 hours

Some of the lentils and smaller beans do not require soaking. The cooking times are:

Brown lentils	35–40 minutes
Split peas (yellow and green)	45 minutes
Split red lentils	20–30 minutes
Mung beans	45 minutes

Grains

All grains may be cooked by the basic method of boiling in water or, better still for a savoury dish, vegetable stock (see page 73 for method of making vegetable stock). Once cooked, they can then be prepared according to the recipe.

Cooking chart

Grain	Amount raw	Liquid	Boiling time	Yield
Barley	1 cup	3–4 cups	45 mins	3 cups
Buckwheat	1 cup	2 cups	20 mins	3 cups
Bulghur	1 cup	2 cups	15 mins	2½ cups
Millet	1 cup	3 cups	25 mins	4 cups
Rice	1 cup	2 cups	40 mins	3 cups
Wheat	1 cup	3½ cups	60 mins	2½ cups
Rye	1 cup	3½ cups	60 mins	2½ cups

You will find that different varieties of the same grain vary in their cooking time and the amount of liquid they absorb. Check towards the end of the cooking time and if necessary add a little boiling water.

Basic cooking method

Rinse the raw grain in a sieve. Place in a saucepan with the measured volume of liquid. Bring to the boil, turn the heat to simmer and cover with a well-fitting lid.

Ten minutes before the cooking time is up, remove the lid and test the grain. It should be tender but still chewy. Turn off the heat, replace the lid and allow to stand for a few minutes.

For convenience you can cook extra grain and store it for 1–2 days in the fridge to incorporate in another dish. Remember you can always add cooked grains to bread mixtures, cakes, soups, nut roasts, burgers, and salads. If your grains have been cooked in water rather than stock you can make them into delicious breakfast dishes.

Sautéed grain

Another way to cook grain is to melt a little ghee in a saucepan, add a chopped onion and some spices or herbs. Stir in your measured amount of grain and sauté for a few minutes. Now add the measured volume of liquid, put the lid on the pan and continue as for the basic boiling method above.

Vegetable stock

We prepare a vegetable stock before each meal from ingredients accumulated when preparing the previous meal. For instance, when making the salads and cleaning the vegetables for lunch we put into a bowl all the offcuts of the vegetables so that when we come to cook the evening meal everything is ready. These can be the tough green ends of leeks, the skins of onions, the ends of carrots, the outer leaves of cabbage. We also use the peelings from tough root vegetables such as kohl rabi and celeriac. We sometimes also include orange and lemon skins and even the leaf end of a pineapple, which may sound strange but it gives a lovely flavour! Of course all these bits and pieces have been really well cleaned and any bad bits removed.

If you have not got these sort of things saved then of course you can make stock by selecting such vegetables as carrot, onion, turnip and leek and cleaning them and chopping into chunks.

Place all these bits and pieces in a saucepan with plenty of water and herbs, bring to simmering point, cover with a lid and maintain a gentle simmer for about an hour. Strain the liquid and save. This is your stock. You can now go ahead and use it to cook beans, grains, soups and sauces. It's best to use your stock fairly soon as after a few hours it will develop a sour flavour. There is no reason why you shouldn't freeze some stock to keep for later use if that will help you, but it is a good idea to get into the habit of making it regularly.

Seaweeds

Seaweed (or sea vegetables) are very well worth including in your diet, as they contain valuable trace elements and vitamins. In many parts of the world they have been used for thousands of years and have only recently become disregarded here in Britain – although you can still find traditional delicacies such as laver bread in West Wales.

Seaweed is known to combat radiation in the body. After the Second World War it was noticed among the survivors of the bombings of Hiroshima and Nagasaki that the survivors who had regularly eaten seaweeds as part of their traditional Japanese diet did not develop cancer as a result of the exposure to radiation to the same extent as people who did not eat seaweed. In these days of nuclear disasters this in itself is enough to recommend the inclusion of seaweed in the diet.

Because of our polluted coastal waters I do not recommend that you gather your own seaweeds but buy packets of dried seaweed which will have been harvested in pure water. As some of these seaweeds will have brine adhering to them it is necessary to rinse them well.

The varieties that we regularly use are as follows:

Nori   This comes in sheet form and requires no rinsing. Toast very briefly (10 seconds) either under a hot grill or over a gas flame. It can then be used to make sushi (rolls filled with cooked rice and vegetables), or you can just crumble the toasted Nori and use it as a garnish.

Kombu   Wash and chop a piece and add to beans during cooking to give flavour and to soften the beans.

Hiziki and arame   These should be well rinsed and soaked for about 30 minutes, then simmered with a little grated fresh ginger root and chopped onion to add to cooked rice. They are also delicious added to grated root salads.

Wakame   Rinse and soak for 10 minutes before mixing with sautéed vegetables, or add to soups.

Agar agar flakes   These flakes are totally bland. They require no rinsing. Use them to make a delicious jelly by dissolving in boiling fruit juice. The jelly can then be used with fruit salads or trifles or fruit tarts.

Herbs and spices

As you are no longer using salt, you will find that you will use more herbs and spices than perhaps you used to to give more flavour to your dishes. This is an area in which you can really develop your creativity. Get into the habit of tasting your dish and smelling your little jars of herbs to find flavours which will enhance, lift, complement the recipe. I've included suggestions for the herbs and spices in all my savoury recipes but these can all be changed and you may find that you have different preferences. Don't use too many herbs in one dish – one or two will be sufficient and then you will be able to identify each one, and bank it in your taste memory to refer to and use another day. Whole books have been written about herbs and spices. I will just give some brief advice and list the ones we use the most frequently.

Herbs

It is lovely to grow your own herbs and to be able to use them fresh. If you have no garden you can easily grow a few varieties in pots on the window sill or out on the balcony or patio. When the flowers are about to open and the volatile oil (the flavour) is at its strongest, pick bunches, tie them up with string and hang them in the kitchen away from steam. When they are really dry, strip the leaves from the stalks, crumble and put into clean, labelled jars to use through the winter.

Of course you can readily buy herbs. It is best to buy them loose in small quantities from your wholefood shop. Replace them frequently as they soon lose their flavour. They should be kept in a cool, dark cupboard.

Here is a list of our favourites:

Basil	Savoury
Marjoram	Tarragon
Mint	Chives
Oregano	Sage
Fennel	Bay leaf
Dill	Coriander
Thyme	Parsley
Rosemary	Lovage

Spices

We enjoy using the milder curry spices in our cooked dishes

and in salad dressings. They give a lot of flavour and an exotic touch to what may be a very simple dish. We don't use any of the hot curry spices such as cayenne pepper or chilli as these are quite aggravating to the digestive tract.

Rather than buying curry powder, which will also contain the hot spices, I suggest you buy the individual spices. These can then be used separately in the dish and you will become familiar with their flavours and be able to create your own curry-style dishes flavoured to your taste.

The ones we use are:

Coriander	Mustard seed
Cumin	Cinnamon
Fenugreek	Ginger
Cardomom	Star anise
Sweet paprika	Clove
Black pepper	

Ghee

If you have glanced through the recipes you will probably have noticed that the fat which we use is always ghee. It is better than cooking oil, which can produce carcinogens when overheated. It is also preferable to margarine, which is very highly processed and often contains additives. Do always use ghee very sparingly as your intake of fats should be low.

Ghee is butter which has been clarified. It is very easy to make and preferable to bought ghee. The process of clarification removes the animal proteins, unstable fats and the water so it will not go rancid and will keep in the fridge for a long time.

To begin with, make just a small amount of ghee – say two 8oz (225g) packs of butter. When you are familiar with the process you can then make quite a lot, perhaps eight or ten packs, and pour the ghee into ceramic or glass containers (jam jars serve quite well for this). You can store these at the back of the fridge and that is then one job out of the way.

To make ghee

Put the butter into a saucepan (stainless steel, of course) and melt over a very low heat. A foam will rise to the surface. Skim off the foam and discard – a perforated spoon is useful for skimming. You will notice that the oil is still cloudy. Still on a very low heat, allow the melted butter to simmer gently. When more foam rises skim it off again. Keep watching it and you will see that the oil will become clear and you will be able to see a sediment on the bottom of the pan. This will accumulate into granules. When the oil is perfectly clear, remove it from the heat. Allow to cool a little and then pour through a fine sieve into containers. It should be golden yellow in colour. You will find that you have in fact discarded very little of the original amount of butter.

Uses for ghee

For sautéeing vegetables.
For making sauces by the roux method.
In bread and cake making.
For crumble toppings.
For pastry making (use about one quarter of ghee to flour).
For greasing tins prior to filling with a baking mixture.

SOUP RECIPES

Green Pea Soup

1 cup (8oz/250g) split peas
4 cups (1¾ pints/1 litre) or
    more vegetable stock
1–2 carrots, cut into
    matchsticks
1 onion, chopped
1–2 potatoes, finely diced

1 clove garlic, crushed
1 teaspoon ghee
pinch dried tarragon
pinch ground coriander or a
    few sprigs fresh
1 teaspoon cider vinegar

Simmer the peas in the stock until tender (about 40 minutes). Sauté the vegetables and garlic in the ghee with the herbs until soft. Add the cooked split peas, the stock and the cider vinegar. Add more vegetable stock if needed. Simmer gently for a few minutes. Serve with wholemeal bread (still warm if possible) or mixed grain loaf.

Carrot and Lentil Soup

1 cup (8oz/250g) red lentils, washed
4 cups (1¾ pints/1 litre) vegetable stock
6 carrots, cut into matchsticks
1 teaspoon ghee

3 tomatoes
2 teaspoons cider vinegar
1 clove garlic
1 onion, chopped
1 teaspoon dried dill, weed or seed
½ teaspoon dried fennel

Simmer the washed lentils in the vegetable stock until soft (about 30 minutes). While these are cooking, sauté the carrot pieces in the ghee. Then add them to the lentils and continue cooking.

In the blender put the tomatoes, cider vinegar, garlic, onion and herbs and blend well. Add this mixture to the lentils. Cook for a further 10 minutes. Serve with slices of wholewheat bread.

Lettuce and Potato Soup

1 teaspoon ghee
1–2 onions, sliced
1–2 potatoes, chopped
2 lettuces, roughly chopped

2 cups (18 fl oz/500 ml) vegetable stock
1 cup (8 fl oz/250 ml) soya milk
watercress sprigs
chives, finely chopped

Melt the ghee in a saucepan and add the onions and potatoes. Sauté for a few minutes. Add the chopped lettuce and continue to sauté for 5 more minutes.

Add the stock and bring to the boil, cover the pan and simmer for 15 minutes. Cool for a few minutes and then blend. Reheat and add the soya milk. Serve sprinkled with the watercress sprigs and the chives.

Kathleen's Winter Soup

2 tablespoons (½oz/15g) wholemeal flour
1 tablespoon sweet paprika
3¾ cups (1½ pints/900ml) vegetable stock
4 tomatoes, sliced

1 cup (4oz/100g) white cabbage, finely chopped
2 leeks, sliced
2–3 carrots, thinly sliced
1 teaspoon mixed dried herbs

Sift together the flour and paprika and add a little stock, mixing to form a thick paste. Bring the remaining stock to the boil, stir a little into the paste and return to the pan. Bring back to the boil, stirring. Add the vegetables and herbs, cover and simmer for 40 minutes.

You may need to adjust the thickness of this soup by adding a little more stock.

Parmentier (clear vegetable soup)

1 tablespoon ghee
2 large carrots, chopped into ½ inch (1 cm) pieces
1 stick celery, sliced
1 medium onion, finely chopped
6 outer cabbage leaves, cut into thin strips

2–3 potatoes, cubed
3¾ cups (1½ pints/900ml) vegetable stock
1 level teaspoon low salt yeast extract
1 teaspoon marjoram

Melt the ghee in a saucepan. Add the carrots, celery, onion and cabbage. Cook over a low heat for 10 minutes, stirring frequently.

Add the potato cubes and continue to cook for a further 5 minutes. Add 1¼ cups (½ pint/300 ml) of vegetable stock and simmer until the vegetables are just tender. Add the rest of the stock, yeast extract and marjoram and cook for 1 minute.

Minestrone Soup

½ cup (3½oz/90g) haricot beans, soaked overnight

6–7 cups (2½–2¾ pints/1.6–1.75 litres) vegetable stock

½ cup (2oz/50g) wholewheat macaroni

1 tablespoon ghee

2 carrots, cut into thin matchsticks

½ stick celery, cut into thin slices

1 onion, cut into thin rings

1 potato, finely diced

2 tomatoes, chopped

1 bay leaf

1 tablespoon fresh chopped parsley

1 teaspoon dried marjoram

few chives, chopped

1–2 cloves garlic, chopped

Cook the beans in 2–3 cups (18–25 fl oz/500–750ml) vegetable stock (about 1 hour).

Cook the pasta in water with the bay leaf (about 15 minutes). Strain. Melt the ghee in a saucepan and add the vegetables. Sauté for about 15 minutes, stirring occasionally. Add the tomatoes, the beans with the stock in which they cooked, the marjoram and the garlic. Add the remaining stock as necessary and simmer for 10 minutes. Serve sprinkled with chopped chives and parsley.

Scotch Broth

½ cup (3½oz/90g) barley
1 dessertspoon ghee
2 carrots, sliced or cubed
1 swede or turnip, finely
  cubed
2 leeks, thinly sliced
2 potatoes, diced

4 cups (1¾ pints/1 litre)
  vegetable stock
1 teaspoon low salt yeast
  extract
½ cup (4oz/100g) goat's milk
  yoghurt

Cook the barley in 3 cups (1¼ pints/750 ml) water until soft (about 1 hour). Melt the ghee in a saucepan and add the vegetables. Sauté for 10 minutes, stirring occasionally. Add half the stock and the yeast extract dissolved in a little boiling water.

Cook gently until all the vegetables are tender. Add the barley with the cooking water and more stock as necessary. Stir in the goat's milk yoghurt, reheat gently and serve.

Cream of Cauliflower Soup

1 medium cauliflower,
  broken into small sprigs,
  stalk finely chopped
2 cups (18 fl oz/500ml)
  vegetable stock
1 tablespoon ghee
2 tablespoons (½oz/15g)
  wholewheat flour

2 cups (18 fl oz/500 ml) soya
  milk
grated nutmeg
chopped fresh parsley to
  garnish

Simmer the cauliflower in the stock until soft (10 minutes). Strain, saving the liquid. Rub the cauliflower through a sieve.

Melt the ghee in a saucepan, add the flour and cook, stirring constantly for 5 minutes. Add the reserved stock and the soya milk and whisk until smooth and thick. Add the cauliflower

and a good grating of nutmeg. Simmer, stirring, for 5 minutes.
Serve sprinkled with chopped parsley.

Brown French Onion Soup

1 tablespoon ghee	black pepper to taste
2–3 onions, thinly sliced	1 level teaspoon grated
1 teaspoon dried basil	nutmeg
4 cups (1¾ pints/1 litre) rich	½ cup (4oz/100g) red lentils
vegetable stock	1 tablespoon cider vinegar
2 bay leaves	1 dessertspoon apple juice
2 cloves garlic, crushed	

Melt the ghee in a saucepan and sauté the onions with the basil
until transparent. Add all the other ingredients and simmer for
30–40 minutes, adding more stock or apple juice if the mixture
appears rather thick.

Serve with wholemeal bread croûtons sautéed in a very little
ghee, or with warm wholemeal bread.

Isle of Wight Soup (a very old traditional recipe
modified for this diet)

1 tablespoon ghee	½ cup (2oz/50g) swede
1 small onion, thinly sliced	2 potatoes, thinly sliced
2 cabbage leaves, thinly sliced	1 teaspoon mixed dried herbs
1–2 carrots, thinly sliced	

Melt the ghee in a saucepan. Add all the vegetables and lay a
piece of greased paper tightly over the top of the vegetables.
Leave to sweat for 15 minutes on a very low heat (you should
be able to put a knife through the paper at this stage).

Remove the paper, add 2½ cup (1 pint/600 ml) cold water
and the herbs. Bring to a simmer and let the vegetables cook

until tender (15 minutes). Blend and return to the pan to reheat. If necessary you can add a little vegetable stock or soya milk to thin the soup.

Beetroot Soup

2 cups (12oz/350g) beetroot, diced
1 cup (4oz/100g) swede, finely diced
1 potato, diced
1 onion, cut into fine rings
1 teaspoon ghee
black pepper
lemon juice to taste

4 cups (1¾ pints/1 litre) vegetable stock (made with plenty of carrot)
½ cup (4oz/100g) goat's milk yoghurt
chopped fresh parsley to garnish

Steam the beetroot until tender. Steam the swede and potato together until soft. Sauté the onion in ghee.

Blend half the beetroot in the stock, and bring to simmering point. Add the onion rings, pepper and lemon juice to taste. At the last minute add the potato, swede and rest of the beetroot (they should retain their individual colours). Put a blob of goat's milk yoghurt into each dish with a sprinkle of parsley.

Cashew and Carrot Soup

You can also serve this soup cold as a summer soup.

½ cup (2oz/50g) onion, chopped
1 cup (8oz/225g) carrot, grated
1 teaspoon ghee
2 tomatoes, chopped
½ cup (2oz/50g) apple, chopped

5 cups (2 pints/1.2 litres) stock
½ cup (3½oz/90g) grain (rice or millet are both good)
a few raisins
½ cup (2oz/50g) cashew nuts
½ cup (4 fl oz/120ml) soya milk (optional)

Sauté the onion and carrot in the ghee until the onion is transparent. Add the tomato, apple, stock, and grain. Simmer until the grain is cooked.

Add the raisins and cashew nuts and simmer for a further 5 minutes. You may add soya milk to make this soup extra rich.

Oatmeal Soup

½ cup (1½oz/40g) jumbo oats or oatmeal (medium or coarse)
1 teaspoon ghee
1 onion, sliced
2 cloves garlic, finely chopped

1 large tomato, chopped
3¾ cups (1½ pints/900 ml) vegetable stock
½ teaspoon dried thyme
½ cup (4 fl oz/120 ml) soya milk

Dry roast the oats in a heavy saucepan. They should be a golden brown colour. Set aside. Add the ghee to the pan and sauté the onion until transparent.

Stir in the oats, garlic, tomatoes, stock and herb. Simmer for about 10 minutes. Add the soya milk, reheat and serve.

COOKED DISH RECIPES

Fabulous Four-layer Bake

1 cup (7oz/200g) tofu (firm variety), cut into cubes
1 dessertspoon cider vinegar
1 teaspoon dried sage
3 cups (12oz/350g) kale, chopped
1 cup (7oz/200g) butter beans, cooked
½ cup (2oz/50g) mushrooms, sliced

½ cup (2oz/50g) cashew nuts, ground
2 tablespoons sesame seeds
1 teaspoon ghee
2 teaspoons caraway seeds
2 tomatoes, chopped
2 teaspoons tahini
1 cup (8 fl oz/250 ml) apple juice

To make the first layer: marinate the tofu in the cider vinegar with the sage for about 1 hour, turning the pieces occasionally. Drain and arrange the tofu in the bottom of an ovenproof dish.

For the second layer: steam the kale for 4 minutes, and arrange on top of the tofu.

For the third layer: add the cooked butter beans to the other layers.

The fourth layer is a sauce. Blend all the remaining ingredients and pour over the layers. Bake at 400°F (200°C/ Gas Mark 6) for about 45 minutes until the sauce is set.

Variations: the tofu can be marinated with stock with a teaspoon of low salt yeast extract and other herbs, e.g. thyme, marjoram, dill.

Other steamed greens in season can be used for the second layer: spring greens, sprouting broccoli, spinach, or sliced green beans.

Other beans to try in place of the butter beans are haricots, blackeyes, flageolets or soya beans.

Buckwheat Pilau

1 teaspoon ghee
1 teaspoon garam masala
1–2 onions, roughly chopped
1 cup (6oz/175g) buckwheat, raw
2 cups (18 fl oz/500 ml) rich vegetable stock
1 tablespoon cider vinegar
2–3 sprigs fresh or 2 teaspoons dried coriander

2–3 cups (12–18oz/350– 500g) potato, cubed
2–3 cups (1–1½lb/450– 750g) carrots, cubed
1 cup (7oz/200g) broad beans, shelled
1 cup (5oz/150g) mixed pumpkin and sunflower seeds, toasted

Melt the ghee in a saucepan, add the garam masala and onion and sauté gently. After a few minutes add the buckwheat and cook gently, stirring occasionally. If you are using dry coriander add it at this stage.

Pour in the cider vinegar and vegetable stock and simmer for 15–20 minutes until the buckwheat is tender.

Meanwhile, steam the vegetables together for about 10 minutes. Mix the steamed vegetables with the buckwheat, adding the toasted seeds and the fresh coriander, if used, finely chopped.

Variations: many other vegetables can be used in this adaptable dish; fresh garden peas, sweetcorn, sprigs of cauliflower, sliced green beans. And, of course, you can make pilau with other grains, for example rice, and millet.

Butter Bean and Beetroot Stew

1 cup (7oz/200g) butter
   beans, raw
2 cups (12oz/350g) beetroot,
   cubed
1 cup (8oz/225g) carrot,
   cubed
1 cup (4oz/100g) apple,
   cubed

2–3 courgettes, sliced
1 teaspoon ghee
½ cup (4 fl oz/120 ml) cider
   vinegar
1 cup (2oz/50g) wheat
   sprouts
1 teaspoon dried basil
1 teaspoon dried oregano

Cook the butter beans in water or stock until soft (about 1½ hours). Steam the beetroot and carrot together for 10 minutes until tender. Steam the apples and courgettes together for 4 minutes. Mix the beetroot, carrot, apples and courgettes with the butter beans, adding the cider vinegar and the wheat sprouts. Add the herbs.

Serve with a boiled grain, e.g. rice or barley.

Variations: turnip or swede can be used instead of the other root vegetables.

Curryish Mushrooms

10 medium sized
  mushrooms, stems
  chopped, caps left whole
1 tablespoon ghee
1 onion, chopped
1 teaspoon fenugreek
1 teaspoon ground cumin
1 teaspoon ground coriander

2 cups (8oz/225g) apple,
  diced
1 cup (7oz/200g) brown rice,
  freshly cooked and hot
1 teaspoon sweet paprika
parsley or coriander to
  garnish

Sauté the mushroom caps in ghee until lightly golden. Set aside. Add a little more ghee to the pan if necessary and in it sauté the onion and the spices until the onion is almost transparent.

Add half the chopped apple and the mushroom stalks and continue to cook for a few minutes. Place the rice in the bottom of a casserole. Cover with the onion and apple mixture and arrange the mushroom caps on top. Sprinkle with the paprika and the rest of the apple. If available sprinkle with fresh parsley leaves or fresh coriander.

Lonely Cannellini Dish

1 cup (7oz/200g) cannellini
  beans, soaked overnight
1 cup (6oz/200g) bulghur
  wheat, raw
1 teaspoon dried rosemary
4 small onions
2 carrots, sliced lengthways
4 Jersusalem artichokes,
  cubed

1½ cups (12 fl oz/350 ml)
  vegetable stock
1 level tablespoon arrowroot
1 teaspoon sweet paprika
1 level teaspoon low salt yeast
  extract
2 cups (18oz/500g) leeks,
  chopped
1 teaspoon ghee

Cook the beans in water until soft. Prepare the bulghur wheat by pouring onto it 1½–2 cups (12–18 fl oz/350–500 ml) boiling water and stirring in the rosemary. Leave to swell and absorb all the water (about 20 minutes). Steam the onions, carrots and artichokes.

To make the sauce blend thoroughly together 1¼ cups (½ pint/300 ml) vegetable stock, the arrowroot, paprika, and yeast extract. Tip this into a saucepan with the rest of the stock, stir, and simmer until thickened.

Sauté the leeks in the ghee for a few minutes and add to the sauce. Add the beans and heat through.

Place the bulghur wheat in a dish and arrange the vegetables on top. Finally, pour on the bean sauce mixture.

Variations: other vegetables can be used in season – cabbage, broccoli, cauliflower, kohl rabi etc.

Use a bed of millet or rice instead of the bulghur wheat.

Try using other beans, e.g. flageolet beans, aduki beans, soya beans, butter beans.

Macaroni with Tofu Cheese Sauce

1 cup (4oz/100g) wholewheat
  macaroni
2 leeks, sliced
1½ cups (10oz/275g) fresh
  shelled broad beans
2 cups (8oz/225g)
  mushrooms, sliced
1 teaspoon ghee
1 cup (7oz/200g) tofu
small tub goat's milk yoghurt
½ cup (4 fl oz/120 ml) soya
  milk

½ cup (4 fl oz/120 ml)
  vegetable stock
pinch of dried tarragon
1 clove garlic or small onion,
  chopped
juice of 1 lemon
1 tablespoon arrowroot
black pepper to taste
1 teaspoon sweet paprika
1 tomato, sliced

Boil the macaroni in water until soft. Steam the leeks and broad beans. Sauté the mushrooms in the ghee. Lightly grease an ovenproof bowl with ghee. Mix together the macaroni and vegetables and put in the bowl.

To prepare the sauce put all the ingredients in the blender and whiz until smooth. Pour over the macaroni and vegetable mixture and arrange the slices of tomato on top. Bake at 375°F (190°C/Gas Mark 5) for about 30 minutes until the sauce is set.

Variations: many other vegetables can be used in season, such as spring greens, sprouting broccoli, sweet corn, spinach, or runner beans.

Barley with Mixed Vegetables

1 cup (7oz/200g) barley, raw
1½ cups (6oz/175g)
    mushrooms, sliced
2 onions, chopped
1 tablespoon ghee
1 cup (8oz/225g) carrot,
    cubed
1 cup (6oz/175g) kohl rabi,
    cubed

1 cup (6oz/175g) beetroot,
    cubed
1½ cups (12 fl oz/350 ml)
    strong vegetable stock
1 tablespoon nut butter or
    tahini
1 teaspoon dried tarragon
1 teaspoon dried oregano
juice of 1 lemon

Boil the barley in water until soft (about 50 minutes). Drain. Lightly sauté the mushrooms and onions in ghee and stir into the barley.

Meanwhile steam the carrot and kohl rabi together and the beetroot separately. To make the sauce heat the vegetable stock, stir in the nut butter, herbs and lemon juice and simmer gently for a few minutes.

Put the barley mixture in a serving bowl, pour the sauce over it and arrange the vegetables on top.

Chestnut Roast

1 cup (4oz/100g) dried
  chestnuts
1 cup (6oz/175g) millet
1 cup (8oz/225g) green or
  brown lentils
1 tablespoon ghee
2–3 onions, chopped
2 tomatoes, sliced
3 medium carrots, cubed

½ teaspoon dried basil
1 teaspoon dried thyme
1 teaspoon black pepper
1 cup (4oz/100g) hazelnuts
  and almonds, coarsely
  ground
1 cup (8 fl oz/250 ml) soya
  milk
1 cup (7oz/200g) tofu, cubed

Soak the chestnuts in water for 2 hours. Then, using the soaking water and more as needed simmer until soft (about 45 minutes).

Cook separately in water or stock the millet (20 minutes) and the lentils (40 minutes). Sauté together in the ghee the onions, tomatoes and carrots, adding the herbs and pepper. Stir together with the millet and lentils in a mixing bowl, adding the hazelnuts and almonds, the soya milk and the roughly chopped chestnuts. Gently add the cubes of tofu.

Put in a greased baking tray, smooth the top and bake at 400°F (200°C/Gas Mark 6) for 30 minutes.

Variation: in the autumn you can use fresh chestnuts. To peel make a small split in each, using a sharp pointed knife. Plunge into boiling water and simmer for 5 minutes. Scoop a few out at a time and peel while still hot. The inner, fluffy skin should come away at the same time. These can then be just roughly chopped and included in the recipe at the end.

Farmhouse Crumble

1 cup (7oz/200g) haricot
   beans, soaked overnight
2 dessertspoons ghee
2 dessertspoons tahini
½ cup (2oz/50g) wholewheat
   flour
1 cup (3oz/75g) jumbo oats
1 tablespoon sesame seeds
1 cup (4oz/100g) hazelnuts,
   ground
1 cup (4oz/100g) leeks or
   onions, sliced

1 cup (4oz/100g) broccoli,
   chopped
1 cup (4oz/100g) cauliflower,
   chopped
½ cup (2oz/50g) celeriac,
   grated
2–3 mushrooms, sliced
1 sharp apple, cubed
1 cup (8 fl oz/250 ml) rich
   vegetable stock
1 tablespoon cider vinegar

Cook the beans in water or extra stock until soft (about 1 hour).

To make the topping: melt the ghee and with the tahini pour on to the flour, oats, sesame seeds and hazelnuts. Stir until well mixed.

To make the base: lightly steam the vegetables and apple together for 6 minutes. Mix with the cooked beans and the stock and cider vinegar. A little liquid from the beans can be added if you wish.

Place this mixture in an ovenproof dish and cover with the topping. Bake at 375°F (190°C/Gas Mark 5) for about 20 to 30 minutes.

Variations: any vegetables in season can be used – peas, sweetcorn, cabbage, whatever you fancy. If you have other cooked beans left over from another dish you can use them instead of the haricots. This is a great use it up dish!

Spiced Chickpeas with Buckwheat

1½ cups (10oz/275g)
  chickpeas, soaked
  overnight
2 teaspoons ghee
1 teaspoon ground cumin
1 teaspoon ground coriander
3 cups (1¼ pints/750ml)
  vegetable stock
4 cardomom pods
2 teaspoons grated fresh root
  ginger

1 cup (8 fl oz/250 ml) apple
  juice
1 onion, chopped
2 cloves garlic, crushed
1 teaspoon dried sage
1 cup (6oz/175g) buckwheat
4 cups (1 lb/450g) spring
  greens, chopped

Boil the chickpeas for 10 minutes and discard the water (as explained in 'Beans and flatulence' on page 70).

Melt the ghee and sauté the cumin and coriander for 5 minutes. Add the drained chickpeas and stock, the cardomom pods, ginger, apple juice, onion, garlic and sage. Simmer. While they are cooking (1–1½ hours) boil the buckwheat until just soft (20 mins). When the chickpeas are tender stir in the buckwheat.

Serve with the greens, lightly steamed for 5 minutes, either separately or gently stirred in.

Variations: this dish can be made with other beans, other grains, and other vegetables! The cooking times for the various beans and grains can be checked on the charts I have given (page 72). So, with experimentation this recipe can adapt to become 20 different dishes.

Dishy Rice with Watercress Sauce

2 cups (14oz/400g) rice
4 carrots, cut into
matchsticks
3 courgettes, cut into
matchsticks
1 teaspoon ghee
½ cup (2oz/50g) cashew nuts
2 onions, chopped
½ cup (2oz/50g) mushrooms,
sliced

2 cups (18 fl oz/500 ml)
vegetable stock
3 tablespoons (¾oz/20g) rice
flour
1 bunch watercress
juice of ½ lemon
1 cup (8 fl oz/250 ml) white
wine
1 teaspoon honey

Boil the rice in 3½ cups (1½ pints/900 ml) water until it is soft and the grains are still separate. Steam the carrots and courgettes (5 minutes). Sauté in ghee the cashew nuts, then the onions and finally the mushrooms, removing and reserving each ingredient separately.

To make the sauce: put all the remaining ingredients in the blender and whiz until smooth. Transfer to a saucepan and simmer for 10 minutes, stirring all the time. The sauce will have thickened.

To serve, mix the onions and the mushrooms with the rice, pour the sauce over, and arrange the steamed vegetables on top. Sprinkle with the cashew nuts.

Variations: of course you can use other vegetables in this dish – steamed beans and peas are nice.

You can use arrowroot instead of rice flour if you wish, but 1 tablespoon will be enough to thicken the sauce.

Baked Beans

1 cup (7oz/200g) haricot
 beans, soaked overnight
2 bay leaves
1/2 cup (3 1/2oz/90g) barley
1 cup (6oz/175g) potatoes,
 cubed
1/2 cup (4 fl oz/120 ml) cider
 vinegar
1 tablespoon molasses

4 tomatoes, chopped
2 teaspoons fenugreek
4 cups (1 3/4 pints/1 litre)
 vegetable stock
1 cup (4oz/100g) onion,
 chopped
1 teaspoon ghee
1 teaspoon dried basil
1 teaspoon dried marjoram

Cook the beans with the bay leaves until almost tender (1 1/4 hours). Boil the barley until almost done (40 minutes). Combine and add the potato. Cook for a further 15 minutes.

Add the cider vinegar, molasses, tomatoes, and fenugreek. Add enough vegetable stock so that the beans are in a thick sauce.

Sauté the onion in ghee with the basil and marjoram and add to the bean mixture. Place in a casserole and bake at 425°F (220°C/Gas Mark 7) for 30 minutes. Serve with steamed vegetables in season. Any leftovers are good on toast the next day.

Stuffed Courgettes in Spicy Sauce

8 courgettes cut in half
 lengthways
1/2 cup (1oz/25g) bean
 sprouts
1/2 cup (1oz/25g)
 breadcrumbs
1/2 cup (2oz/50g) hazelnuts,
 ground
1/2 teaspoon black pepper
1 teaspoon dried tarragon

1/2 teaspoon dried basil
2–3 mushrooms, sliced
2 teaspoons ghee
1 cup (8oz/225g) red lentils
3 cups (1 1/4 pints/750 ml)
 vegetable stock
1 teaspoon garam masala
juice of 1/2 lemon
1 cup (8oz/225g) goat's milk
 yoghurt

Steam the courgettes for 4 minutes. Mix together the bean sprouts, breadcrumbs, nuts, pepper and herbs.

Sauté the mushrooms in half the ghee and add to the mixture. Scoop out the seedy part of the courgettes and stir into the mixture.

Stuff the courgette halves with the mixture. Place in an ovenproof dish.

To make the sauce: boil the lentils in the stock until soft (20 minutes). Melt the remaining ghee and gently sauté the garam masala and add the cooked lentils, draining if necessary. Add the lemon juice and yoghurt. Stir until heated through. Pour over the stuffed courgettes and bake at 350°F (180°C/Gas Mark 4) for 30 minutes. This is good served with a grain salad.

Hummus

2 cups (14oz/400g) chickpeas
2–3 lemons
4 tablespoons tahini
½ cup (4 fl oz/125 ml) olive oil
3–4 cloves garlic, crushed

To garnish:
parsley
lemon slices
paprika

Soak the chickpeas overnight, rinse and drain. Boil them in fresh water until really tender (about 1½ hours). Drain, saving the liquid.

Put the chickpeas into the blender with 1 cup (8 fl oz/250 ml) of the cooking liquid, add the juice of 1 lemon, the tahini, the olive oil and some of the garlic. Blend well. Taste and adjust the seasoning, adding more lemon and garlic as you like. Serve in a pâté dish with sprigs of parsley, lemon slices and a sprinkling of paprika.

This is a delicious lunch dish, served with slices of fresh wholemeal bread and salads. It is also excellent party food or picnic fare and is extremely useful when travelling.

Split Pea Croquettes

2 cups (1 lb/450g) split peas,
  raw
1 cup (6oz/175g) millet
1 cup (8oz/225g) grated
  carrot
1 cup (4oz/100g) onion,
  finely chopped
1/2 teaspoon black pepper

1/4 teaspoon dried sage
1 cup (4oz/100g)
  mushrooms, chopped
4 teaspoons ghee
1 cup (2oz/50g) wholemeal
  breadcrumbs
1 teaspoon sweet paprika

Cook the split peas until mushy. Cook the millet separately. Drain and mix together with the carrot, onion, pepper and sage. Sauté the mushrooms lightly in a little of the ghee and add to the mixture.

Sprinkle the breadcrumbs and paprika on a board. Take small handfuls of the mixture, shape into balls and roll in the crumb mixture. Lightly sauté them in ghee and place on a baking tray. Bake at 375°F (190°C/Gas Mark 5) for 20 minutes. Serve with a rich gravy or a brown sauce.

Variations: if you have any okara (see page 29) you can add some with the millet. You can use 1/2 cup (2oz/50g) ground hazelnuts with the breadcrumbs.

Millet and Aduki Bean Patties

1 cup (6oz/175g) millet
1 cup (7oz/175g) aduki
  beans, soaked overnight
4 cups (13/4 pints/1 litre)
  vegetable stock
3 carrots, grated

1 teaspoon dried basil
2 teaspoon dried sage
1/2 teaspoon low salt yeast
  extract
1–2 onions, chopped
1 tablespoon ghee

Cook the millet and aduki beans separately in the stock. The beans will take about 30 minutes longer than the millet. Drain off any excess liquid and reserve. Put the millet and beans in a large mixing bowl. Add the grated carrot, the herbs and the yeast extract, dissolved in a small amount of hot stock.

Sauté the onions in the ghee and add to the mixture. Mix well together.

Take out large spoonfuls and make into patty shapes in your hands. Place them on a baking tray that has been lightly greased with ghee.

Bake at 375°F (190°C/Gas Mark 5) oven for 30 minutes. Serve with lentil gravy.

Lentil Gravy

4 cup (4oz/100g) red split
   lentils
1½ cups (12 fl oz/350 ml)
   vegetable stock (or more)

½ teaspoon dried thyme
2 tomatoes
1 garlic clove

Simmer the lentils in the stock with the thyme until soft. Blend with the tomatoes and garlic and a little more liquid if necessary.

Green Pie

⅔ cup (6oz/175g) ghee
2 cups (8oz/225g)
   wholewheat flour
a little spring water
2 onions, chopped
1 teaspoon ghee
4–6 leaves Swiss chard
1 cup (7oz/200g) tofu
juice of 1 lemon

1 level tablespoon arrowroot
1–2 cloves garlic
¼ cup (1oz/25g) almonds,
   ground
⅔ cup (¼ pint/150 ml) soya
   milk
¼ cup (1oz/25g) almonds,
   whole

Make pastry by rubbing the ghee into the flour and adding a little spring water to hold it together. Roll it out and line a pie dish. Bake it blind at 375°F (190°C/Gas Mark 5) for 10 minutes.

Sauté the onions in 1 teaspoon ghee and put into the partly cooked pastry base. Cut the white central ribs from the Swiss chard, slice them and steam for 5 minutes. Add to the onions.

Roughly chop the green leaf of the chard and steam it for 5 minutes. Put into the blender with the tofu, lemon juice, arrowroot, garlic, ground almonds and soya milk. Blend to a thick, green cream. Pour into the pie and decorate with the whole almonds. Bake at 400°F (200°C/Gas Mark 6) for about 45 minutes.

Eat hot or cold. You will find that the filling sets more on cooling.

Variations: other delicious green pies can be made in the same way using spinach, watercress, green peas, broad beans, or calabrese, all with their own delicate individual flavour. You could make a pink pie instead, using tomatoes and a red pepper.

Butter Beans with Rice Flour Sauce

2 cups (14oz/400g) butter beans, soaked overnight
6 cups (2½ pints/1.5 litres) vegetable stock
1½ cups (12oz/350g) tomatoes, chopped
½ cup (½oz/15g) fennel tops (the ferny spray from the top of fennel root)

½ cup (2oz/50g) rice flour
4 tablespoons cider vinegar
1 cup (8oz/225g) carrots, sliced
1 cup (4oz/100g) fennel root, sliced
1 cup (4oz/100g) onion, chopped
2 teaspoons ghee

Cook the butter beans in 4 cups (1¾ pints/1 litre) of the stock until soft (1 to 1½ hours). To make the sauce: blend the tomatoes and fennel tops in the remaining stock. Mix the rice flour to a paste with a little water and stir into the blend. Simmer gently until thickened. Add a little cider vinegar to taste.

Steam the carrots and fennel root together (8 minutes). Sauté the onion in a little ghee. Add these vegetables to the sauce mix.

Pour over the beans and serve with a grain such as millet.

Lentils, Wheatgrains and Rice

1 cup (7oz/200g) rice
1 cup (8oz/225g) green or
   brown lentils
3/4 cup (6oz/175g)
   wheatgrains
1 cup (8oz/225g) goat's milk
   yoghurt

1/2 cup (3 1/2oz/90g) tahini
2 tablespoons cider vinegar
juice of 1 lemon
2 cloves garlic
1 tablespoon sweet paprika

Boil the rice, lentils and wheat separately. Start off with the wheat, which will take about 1 hour, then the rice (40 minutes) and finally the lentils (30 minutes).

Meanwhile prepare the sauce: blend together the yoghurt, tahini, vinegar, lemon juice, garlic and paprika. Adjust the seasonings to taste. Gently heat the sauce and combine with the cooked grains and pulse. Serve with lots of steamed vegetables.

Variations: you can use barley instead of wheat in this dish. They both take the same amount of time to cook.

You could also try beans instead of the lentils, adjusting the cooking time to suit the variety. Aduki beans go very well in this dish.

Lentil Loaf

1 cup (3oz/75g) jumbo oats
1 cup (2oz/50g) chickpea
  sprouts
1 tablespoon ghee
1 large onion, chopped
½ teaspoon ground
  coriander
¾ cup (6oz/175g) lentils
2 cups (18 fl oz/500 ml)
  vegetable stock

1 teaspoon dried sage
1 teaspoon dried basil
2 teaspoons sweet paprika
1 clove garlic, finely chopped
  or crushed
2–3 sticks celery, chopped
1 tablespoon sesame seeds

Line the base of a greased baking tray with the oats mixed with the chickpea sprouts.

Melt the ghee in a saucepan and sauté the onion with the coriander for 5 minutes. Add the lentils and stock and simmer until the lentils are soft (30 minutes), adding more liquid if necessary.

While they are cooking add the herbs, paprika, garlic and the celery. Mix well and pour this mixture on to the base. Sprinkle with the sesame seeds. Bake at 400°F (200°C/Gas Mark 6) for 30 minutes.

This dish is delicious served with one of our chutneys or the C.H.C. sauce (see page 132).

Chinese Sweet and Sour Vegetables

2–3 carrots, cut into
matchsticks
6 spring onions, cut into 1 in
(2.5 cm) lengths
1 cup (4oz/100g) celeriac, cut
into tiny cubes or strips or
2–3 sticks celery, cut into 1
in (2.5 cm) chunks
1 cup (4oz/100g) cauliflower,
broken into small florets
8 Hunza apricots, soaked for
about 8 hours

2½ cups (1 pint/600 ml)
stock, best if this has
included some orange peel
juice of 3 oranges, the juice
and the zest of 1
juice of 1 lemon
grated rind of 1 orange
small piece fresh root ginger,
grated
1 tablespoon arrowroot
1 teaspoon honey
½ cup (2oz/50g) cashew
nuts, lightly toasted

Lightly steam the vegetables together until just tender (about 8 minutes). Remove the stones from the Hunza apricots and cut the fruit in half.

To make the sauce: put in the blender the stock, fruit juices and grated rind, the ginger, arrowroot and honey. Blend all together until smooth. Transfer to a saucepan and gently simmer, stirring all the time until the mixture thickens.

Taste the sauce and adjust the flavour by adding more honey or lemon or orange juice. It should taste both sweet and sour. Add the steamed vegetables and apricots to the sauce and warm them through.

Serve on a bed of boiled rice with the toasted cashew nuts sprinkled on top. This dish goes very well with a salad that includes watercress.

Wheat Barley and Cabbage

1 cup (7oz/200g) wheat
  grains
1 cup (7oz/200g) barley
  grains
4 cups (1¾ pints/1 litre) rich
  vegetable stock
1 cup (8 fl oz/ 250 ml) apple
  juice
½ teaspoon dried thyme
1 teaspoon dried dill seeds
1 tablespoon cider vinegar

2 tomatoes, chopped
2 apples, chopped
½ cup (1oz/25g) sunflower
  seed sprouts
1 teaspoon sweet paprika
2 tablespoons ghee
1–2 onions, chopped
2–3 cups (12oz/350g)
  cabbage, shredded
1 teaspoon caraway seeds

Boil the wheat and barley together in the stock and apple juice
with the herbs and cider vinegar. Add the tomatoes and apples
towards the end of the cooking time (1 hour). Stir in the
sunflower seed sprouts. Pile into a serving dish and sprinkle
with paprika.

Sauté the onion in ghee for about 5 minutes then add the
cabbage and continue to cook for 8 minutes until the cabbage
is tender. Stir in the caraway seeds and serve with the grain
dish.

Cottage Pie

1 cup (8oz/225g) brown
  lentils
2½ cups (1 pint/600 ml)
  vegetable stock
1 teaspoon cider vinegar
1 large onion, chopped
2 medium carrots, sliced
1 teaspoon ghee

1 teaspoon dried oregano
1 teaspoon dried basil
2 tomatoes, chopped
black pepper
3–4 potatoes, cubed
2 tablespoons soya milk
3–4 spring onions or chives,
  chopped

Cook the lentils in the vegetable stock with the cider vinegar until soft (35 to 40 minutes). Sauté the onions and carrots in the ghee along with the herbs, about 10 minutes. Add the tomatoes and cook for a few minutes more. Stir into the lentil mixture, adding black pepper to taste. Put the mixture into an ovenproof dish.

Meanwhile steam the potato until soft (8–10 minutes). Mash with the soya milk and spring onions or chives (or you can make a very creamy mashed potato in the food processor or blender).

Spoon the potato over the lentil mixture and spread it evenly with a fork. Put into a medium oven or under the grill until the top is slightly brown and crispy. Cottage pie is very good served with a chutney (see pages 132–3) or C.H.C. sauce (see page 132).

Butter Bean and Chestnut Casserole

1 cup (7oz/200g) butter beans, soaked overnight
4 cups (1¾ pints/1 litre) vegetable stock
1 cup (4oz/100g) dried chestnuts, soaked overnight
1 cup (8 fl oz/250 ml) apple juice
juice of 1 lemon

2–3 potatoes, cubed
1 cup (4oz/100g) celeriac, grated
1 teaspoon dried mint
½ teaspoon dried star anise
1 clove garlic, crushed
1 cup (8oz/250g) goat's milk yoghurt
1 teaspoon blue poppy seeds (optional)

Simmer the beans in fresh water for 10 minutes, discard the water and add the stock. Simmer until the beans are soft but still whole (1¼ hours).

Cook the chestnuts in the fruit juices, adding water as necessary (don't let them dry out). When cooked chop them roughly. Steam the potatoes until tender (10 minutes).

Mix together the beans, chestnuts and the grated celeriac, adding the mint, star anise, and garlic. Combine with the yoghurt and gently heat through.

Put the mixture in a casserole and cook in the oven at 375°F (190°C/Gas Mark 5) for about 20 minutes. You can sprinkle with the blue poppy seeds if you wish.

Creamy Yellow Macaroni

1 cup (8oz/225g) yellow split peas

3 cups (1¼ pints/750 ml) vegetable stock

½ cup (2oz/50g) cashew nuts

1 cup (8oz/250g) goat's milk yoghurt

½ teaspoon grated nutmeg

1 level tablespoon fresh coriander, chopped or 1 teaspoon fresh mint, chopped or ½ teaspoon dried mint

½ cup (2oz/50g) wholewheat macaroni

Simmer the split peas in the stock until very soft. Add the cashew nuts towards the end of the cooking time (30–40 minutes). Stir in the goat's milk yoghurt, nutmeg and herbs.

Boil the macaroni in water, drain when tender and add the pasta to the split pea mixture. Place in an ovenproof dish and cook in the oven at 375°F (190°C/Gas Mark 5) for 20 minutes. Serve with plenty of steamed vegetables.

Tofu Quiche

3/4 cup (6oz/175g) ghee
2 cups (8oz/250g)
    wholewheat flour
spring water, chilled
1–2 onions, sliced
a little ghee for frying
2 cups (8oz/250g) greens,
    finely chopped
1½ cups (10oz/275g) tofu
    (firm)
1 cup (8oz/250g) goat's milk
    yoghurt
½ cup (4 fl oz/120 ml) soya
    milk

1 tablespoon arrowroot
juice of 1 lemon
3–4 spring onions, roughly
    chopped
1–2 cloves garlic, crushed
1 teaspoon dill weed
½ teaspoon celery seeds
black pepper
½ teaspoon white mustard
    seed, ground
2 tomatoes, sliced

Make pastry by rubbing the ghee into the flour and adding a little spring water to bind it. Roll out and line a large quiche dish. Bake blind at 375°F (190°C/Gas Mark 5) for 5 minutes.

Sauté the onions in a little ghee until transparent. Put them in the pastry case. Steam the greens for 5 minutes, and arrange on top of the onions.

In the blender put the tofu, yoghurt, soya milk, arrowroot, lemon juice, spring onions, garlic, herbs, and seasoning and blend well. Pour this mixture into the quiche. Arrange the tomato slices on top. Bake at 375°F (190°C/Gas Mark 5) for 40 minutes until the sauce has set. Eat hot or cold with salad. Variations: use whatever greens are in season to make this lovely quiche. Our favourites are sea kale, calabrese, spring cabbage, purple sprouting broccoli, and spinach.

6

The Dessert

At the Cancer Help Centre we serve a dessert after both lunch and dinner. It's up to you whether you do this or not. If you are feeling comfortably full after eating your salad and cooked dish then there is no need also to eat a dessert. Perhaps you would prefer to eat fruit mid-morning and with your after-noon tea. One more thing to consider is that if you are suffering from an acid stomach as a result of eating large quantities of raw vegetables it may be helpful to separate fruit and salads and eat them at different meals. Experiment and find out what suits you best.

Fruits

When buying fruits, follow the same guidelines that I gave you for buying vegetables. You should try to obtain organically grown, local fruits whenever possible. You can also enjoy citrus fruits such as lemons, oranges, grapefruits and tangerines. It is now possible to buy these unsprayed, usually from Israel. Look out for organically grown grapes; they are wonderful, with a much better flavour than the non-organic ones.

Dried fruits are a useful addition, particularly in the winter. A lot of dried fruits are preserved with sulphur which is obviously not good. It is always possible to find sun-dried alternatives. To prevent vine fruits from sticking together in transit they are often sprayed with oil, and sometimes mineral oil is used – again, obviously a bad idea. If a vegetable oil has been used it is usually a low grade one and so place the fruit in a sieve and rinse with plenty of hot water before using them. Avoid tropical dried fruits such as bananas and pineapple. They are covered with preservatives with 'E' additives.

Look out for Hunza apricots. These hard dried fruits are sun-dried in Afghanistan where they are grown by the Hunza people, well known for their longevity. After soaking the fruits for a few hours or overnight they are really delicious and require no cooking. Occasionally you can crack open the nut inside and eat the almond-flavoured kernel. Growing alongside the apricots in Afghanistan are mulberries. We buy these in their sun-dried form and make jams and sauces from them, as well as adding them to fruit crumble mixes. They taste like a strongly flavoured blackberry. Sun dried figs and dates are useful. We make a 'jam' from them by simply blending them with a little water or fruit juice. They are also good for adding fruit sugars to cakes and desserts. Just chop them up small and simmer in a little water until soft. You can then blend them or simply add them to your recipe as they are.

Remember that if you are using the peel of citrus fruits that have not been grown organically it is important to scrub the skin really well in water that has a little vinegar in it. This should remove the chemical sprays and waxes.

Nuts

Nuts are a useful addition to desserts. You should buy them really fresh as the oils in nuts soon go rancid. This is especially so with walnuts and brazil nuts. It is best to buy these at their harvest time still in their shells and to crack them as you need them. Almonds and hazel nuts are good as they keep their inner skin which helps to preserve their freshness. Cashew nuts are lovely, but they do need to be fresh – check when buying them.

Fruit Salads

It will be obvious to you that to comply with the diet the best form of dessert to eat regularly is fresh fruit. Fruit salad is the obvious choice. It seems unnecessary to give recipes for fruit salads as it seems impossible to find a combination that isn't delicious! However, let me give you a few ideas for ringing the changes from the fruit salad in which everything is simply chopped into small pieces.

Try varying the textures of your fruit desserts. As well as chopping your chosen fruits you can also slice, grate and blend them. These various textures can then be combined by spooning into bowls in layers.

Play with colour. Make two different blends of contrasting colours – perhaps a golden yellow one made by blending apricots with tofu, the other apples blended with blackcurrant to give a deep purple colour. Spoon these blends in layers into clear glass bowls or sundae glasses and top with a few grated almonds. It looks amazing and tastes wonderful too!

Fruit to choose from for your fresh fruit desserts

apples	bananas	pears	grapes
oranges	satsumas	mandarins	tangerines
kiwi fruit	lemons	grapefruit	nectarines
mangoes	apricots	strawberries	raspberries
loganberries	blackcurrants	gooseberries	redcurrants
pineapples	melons*	figs	plums
peaches	guava	greengages	

* Melons can be a little indigestible when combined with other fruit. Perhaps this is why they are traditionally eaten alone as a starter.

There are recipes for creams and sauces which you will enjoy serving with your fresh fruit salads on pages 117–118. Remember that you can make lovely jellies from agar agar flakes and fruit juice.

DESSERT RECIPES

Some of these recipes are quite complicated and quite a few are cooked. They are for more occasional use, perhaps for a dinner party or special occasion.

The Perfect Pear

4 pears
1 cup (6oz/175g) dates
grated rind and juice of 2
    oranges

½ teaspoon cinnamon
1 cup (8 fl oz/250 ml) spring
    water

Cut the pears in half lengthways and steam until soft. Carefully transfer to a serving dish.

In a saucepan put the dates, the rind and juice of the oranges, cinnamon and water. Simmer gently until the dates are soft. Blend. Pour this sauce over the pears and bake at 375°F (190°C/Gas Mark 5) for 20 minutes. Serve hot or cold with cashew or almond cream (see page 117).

Banana Split

4 bananas
2 cups (18 fl oz/500 ml)
    spring water
1½ cups (12 fl oz/350 ml)
    soya milk
1 tablespoon arrowroot

1 teaspoon carob powder
1 tablespoon honey
1 cup (4oz/100g) cashew nuts
½ cup (2oz/50g) chopped
    hazelnuts

Place the peeled bananas in an ovenproof serving dish. Put 1 cup (8 fl oz/250 ml) spring water and 1 cup (8 fl oz/250 ml) soya milk in a saucepan and heat. Cream together the arrowroot and carob powder with a little water and add to the heated liquid. Stir and heat gently until the mixture thickens. Add the honey, stir and pour the mixture over the bananas.

Make a cashew cream by first grinding the cashews and then blending them with the remaining soya milk and spring water. Pour this cream on top of the other ingredients, sprinkle with the chopped nuts and bake at 350°F (180°C/Gas Mark 4) for 20 minutes.

Bliss Balls

1 cup (6oz/175g) dates, chopped small
½ cup (4 fl oz/120 ml) spring water
grated rind and juice of 1 lemon
grated rind and juice of 1 orange
1 teaspoon ground cinnamon
⅔ cup (3oz/75g) almonds, ground
½ cup (1½oz/40g) jumbo oatflakes
1½ cups (5oz/150g) desiccated coconut

Simmer the dates in the water with the grated rind and juice of the orange and lemon and the cinnamon. When the dates are soft put them in a bowl with the almonds, the oatflakes and half the coconut and mix together. The mixture should be fairly stiff. If too sticky add more flakes, if too dry add a little fruit juice.

Roll tablespoons of the mixture into balls in your hands and then roll in the rest of the coconut. Chill for a while before serving.

Jelly, Fruit and Cream

2½ cups (1 pint/600 ml) apple juice
2 teaspoons agar agar
grated rind and juice of 1 orange
3 peaches
½ cup (2oz/50g) redcurrants
½ cup (2oz/50g) cashew nuts
¼ cup (1½oz/40g) tofu
1 cup (8 fl oz/250 ml) soya milk
grated rind of 1 lemon
1 teaspoon honey

To make the jelly: heat the apple juice in a pan and stir in the agar agar flakes until completely dissolved. Add the grated rind and juice of the orange.

Slice the peaches and arrange in a serving bowl. Pour the jelly over them, sprinkle with the redcurrants and put aside to set.

Make a cashew cream by grinding the nuts, then putting them in the blender with the tofu, soya milk, grated rind of the lemon and the honey. Blend well (the cream should be quite thick). Decorate the jelly with blobs of the cream, or pipe the cream on for a special effect.

Variations: lots of other fruits can be used in the jelly, such as raspberries, strawberries, slices of apple, pears, fresh apricots, or lightly steamed gooseberries. Almond cream is also delicious with it (page 117).

Apricot Cream Pie

1 cup (4oz/100g) wholewheat
  flour
1 cup (3oz/75g) fine or
  medium oatmeal
3 teaspoons tahini
½ cup (4oz/100g) ghee
1 tablespoon malt extract

1 cup (6oz/175g) Hunza
  apricots, soaked
½ cup (4 fl oz/120 ml) soya
  milk
1 tablespoon arrowroot
1 cup (7oz/200g) firm tofu
2 bananas

Make the pastry base by mixing together the flour and oatmeal, rubbing in the tahini and ghee and stirring in the malt extract. Press this mixture into a baking dish to make a pastry shell and bake blind at 375°F (190°C/Gas Mark 5) for 20 minutes. Stone the apricots and put the fruit into the pastry base.

Blend the soya milk, arrowroot, tofu and bananas together, adding a little of the apricot soaking juice if the blend is very thick, but don't make it too runny. Pour into the pastry case and bake at 400°F (200°C/Gas Mark 6) for 30 minutes. As it cools the filling will set firmer.

Variations: try other fruit in this pie – pears with a squeeze of lemon and some sultanas are good.

Date, Nut and Banana Pie

½ cup (4oz/100g) ghee
1½ cups (6oz/175g) wholewheat flour
a little spring water for binding
½ vanilla pod
1 cup (8 fl oz/250 ml) spring water

1 cup (6oz/175g) dates
½ cup (2oz/50g) cashews, ground
1½ tablespoons arrowroot
2–3 bananas
2 tablespoons desiccated coconut

Make a pastry case by rubbing the ghee into the flour and binding with just enough water to hold it together. Roll it out and line a pie dish. Prick the base and bake it blind at 400°F (200°C/Gas Mark 6) for 15 minutes.

Simmer the vanilla pod in the water for 20 minutes. Remove the pod and add the dates to the water. Cook until soft, then blend with the ground cashews and the arrowroot (you may need to add some more water). Pour this sauce back into the saucepan and stir until it is thick.

Slice the bananas and put into the pastry shell. Pour the sauce over and leave to cool and set. Decorate with the desiccated coconut before serving.

Fruit Crumble

3 apples
3 pears
1/2 cup (3oz/75g) dates
a little spring water
1/2 cup (3oz/75g) sultanas
1 teaspoon ground cloves
1 cup (3oz/75g) medium
    oatmeal

1/2 cup (2oz/50g) cashew
    nuts, ground
1/2 cup (2 1/2oz/65g) sunflower
    seeds
1/2 cup (3oz/75g) sesame
    seeds
1/2 cup (4oz/100g) ghee
1 teaspoon ground cinnamon

Slice the apples and pears and gently simmer with the dates in a little water. Add the sultanas and ground cloves. Grease a pudding dish and put the fruit mixture in.

To make the topping mix together the oatmeal, nuts and seeds and rub in the ghee. Put this mixture over the fruit and dust with the cinnamon.

Bake at 400°F (200°C/Gas Mark 6) for 30 minutes until the topping is cooked.

Orange Fondue

6 oranges
2 apples, chopped
1 banana
1/2 cup (3 1/2oz/90g) tahini
1/2 cup (3 1/2oz/90g) tofu,
    (firm)
1/2 teaspoon ground
    cinnamon

1/2 cup (2 1/2oz/65g) sunflower
    seeds
1 cup (6oz/175g)
    wheatflakes, toasted
1/2 cup (2oz/50g) hazelnuts,
    toasted and chopped

Grate the rind of 4 oranges, peel, and put in pieces in the blender with the rind, chopped apple, banana, tahini, tofu, cinnamon and sunflower seeds. Blend to a thick cream.

Peel the remaining oranges and cut into rounds. Arrange in

individual dishes. Pour the orange cream over them and top
with the wheatflakes and hazelnuts.

Fillet of Millet Pudding

1 cup (6oz/175g) millet
1½ cups (12 fl oz/350 ml)
   apple juice
½ cup (4 fl oz/120 ml) soya
   milk
1 cup (3½oz/90g) stewed
   apple
2–3 bananas, sliced
½ cup (3oz/175g) raisins

½ cup (2oz/50g) cashew
   nuts, ground
grated rind and juice of 1
   lemon
½ teaspoon ground star anise
1 tablespoon malt extract
1 cup (7oz/200g) tofu
1 tablespoon sesame seeds

Cook the millet in 1 cup (8 fl oz/250 ml) of the apple juice and
the soya milk until soft (about 20 minutes). Stir in the stewed
apple, sliced bananas, and raisins and put into a baking dish.
   Blend together the cashew nuts, lemon rind and juice, the
remaining apple juice, star anise, malt extract and tofu. Pour
over the millet mixture. Sprinkle with sesame seeds and bake
at 325°F (160°C/Gas Mark 3) for 30 minutes.

Orange Sunrise

3 oranges
½ cup (3½oz/90g) creamed
   coconut
1 cup (4oz/100g) cashew
   nuts, ground
6 or 8 Hunza apricots, soaked
   for at least 6 hours and
   stoned

2–3 figs, soaked until soft
1 teaspoon ground cinnamon
grated rind of 1 orange
grated rind of 1 lemon
a few grapes, to decorate

Cut the oranges in half and scoop out the pulp. Save the orange shells. Melt the creamed coconut in a bowl over a saucepan of boiling water (it speeds things up a little if you roughly chop the coconut first).

Blend the orange pulp, cashew nuts, soaked fruit, cinnamon and orange and lemon rind. Stir the mixture into the melted coconut. It will set a little as the coconut cools. Spoon the mixture into the orange shells and decorate with the grapes.

Summer Delight Cheese Cake

2 tablespoons ghee
1 tablespoon malt extract
1 cup (3oz/75g) oats
1/3 cup (2oz/50g) raisins
1/2 cup (2oz/50g) chopped
   nuts (almonds, cashews
   etc.)
2 tablespoon tahini
1 cup (6oz/175g) figs, soaked
1 cup (8 fl oz/250 ml) apple
   juice

1 cup (7oz/200g) firm tofu
grated rind and juice of 1–2
   lemons
1 tablespoon arrowroot
1 teaspoon honey
1/4 teaspoon grated nutmeg
1/2 teaspoon ground
   cinnamon
raspberries
redcurrants

Melt the ghee, add the malt extract while still hot and pour into the oats. Add the raisins and nuts and stir. Press into a baking dish and bake at 350°F (180°C/Gas Mark 4) for 30 minutes. Meanwhile blend together the tahini, figs and apple juice. It should be the consistency of runny jam. Spread it over the cooked base.

In the blender put the tofu, grated lemon rind and juice, arrowroot, honey and spices. Blend all together and pour over the base. Bake at 350°F (180°C/Gas Mark 4) for 30 minutes. Decorate with the fruit while cooling.

Variations: apricots or dried mulberries are a good substitute for the figs. Decorate with other fruits in season; orange segments are nice.

TOPPINGS, CREAMS AND SAUCES

As well as making your desserts more delicious these toppings will also increase the protein value of your meal.

Cashew Cream

1 cup (4oz/100g) cashews,   2–3 drops real vanilla essence
    ground
a little spring water, soya
    milk or apple juice

Place in the blender and whiz until smooth, adding the liquid until you get the correct consistency. This topping can be either thick, creamy or quite thin, depending on what you are going to use it on.

Almond Cream

1 cup (4oz/100g) almonds,   1 apricot kernel, ground
    ground   soya milk

Blend all together, using the soya milk to achieve the desired consistency.

Avocado Cream

This is a lovely pale green cream which looks interesting on a fruit salad and amazing piped onto a cheesecake. It tastes good, too!

1 avocado pear, peeled and   a little soya milk or silken
    stoned   tofu
juice of 1/2 lemon

Blend the avocado with the lemon juice and just enough soya milk or tofu to make a stiff cream. Put into a piping bag and swirl on to your dessert.

Tofu Cream

½ cup (3½oz/90g) tofu (firm or silken)
½ cup (1½oz/40g) desiccated coconut

grated rind and juice of ½ lemon
1 teaspoon honey
soya milk

Blend together the tofu, coconut, lemon rind and juice and honey, adding soya milk as needed.

Custard

1 cup (8 fl oz/250 ml) soya milk
1 cup (8 fl oz/250 ml) apple juice

honey to taste
¼ cup (1oz/25g) cornmeal (polenta)
2–3 drops real vanilla essence

Heat together the soya milk and apple juice. Add the honey and stir in the cornmeal and vanilla essence. Cook very gently, stirring constantly, for about 10 minutes. Serve hot or cold.

7

Breads and Cakes

If you are completely new to bread making and are feeling a bit apprehensive, let me reassure you. It's a lovely process and actually very simple. It doesn't take over the kitchen for hours, and the actual handling of the ingredients takes only about 30 minutes. The rest of the time is taken up with the proving (rising) and the cooking and during these times you can be getting on with other things.

Your kitchen needs to be pleasantly warm but not hot and you can prove the dough on a sunny window ledge or near the cooker if it is on. You can even prepare the dough in the evening and leave it overnight in the fridge to make fresh loaves for breakfast.

Don't expect your bread to be like Hovis. Commercially produced bread is cooked with steam, which is why it is so light and fluffy. After eating home-baked bread I think you will find shop bread rather insipid, too light and not as nourishing as the more wholesome home-baked sort.

The basic ingredient of bread is flour and this should be 100 per cent wholemeal flour that has been organically grown, if possible. Nothing has been taken away from this flour; it contains the whole grain, including the bran and the germ. It should be as freshly milled as possible so that it doesn't have time to deteriorate; buy from a store that has a quick turnover where your flour hasn't been sitting on a shelf for months. To increase the protein quality I always add sunflower seeds and sesame seeds to my recipe. This makes the bread a complete protein food. If I have some okara from making soya milk I add a little of this too, or some soya flour.

As we don't add any salt I include a little molasses, which gives a good flavour. Try to buy fresh yeast rather than the dried sort, which I only keep for emergencies. Fresh yeast gives much better results. If your wholefood store doesn't stock it you can probably obtain some from a local baker's shop. You can buy enough to last for a couple of weeks and keep it, wrapped and in an airtight container, in the fridge. Keep your bread in an airtight tin and it will keep fresh for a number of days. I have never frozen my bread but patients tell me that it freezes well, so if you have a freezer you may like to freeze a loaf or two to keep for emergencies.

Sadhya's Bread (basic recipe)

9 cups (2¼ lb/1 kg) wholemeal flour (organic if possible)
½ cup (4oz/100g) ghee, melted
½ cup (3oz/75g) sesame seeds
½ cup (2½oz/65g) sunflower seeds

3¾ cups (1½ pints/900 ml) lukewarm water
1 teaspoon honey
1½oz/40g fresh or 1oz/25g dried yeast
1 tablespoon molasses

Put 6 cups (1½ lb/750g) of the flour into a large bowl. Add the ghee and rub it in with your fingers. Add the sesame and sunflower seeds.

Put 1¼ cups (½ pint/300 ml) of lukewarm water in a jug with the honey and the yeast. Mix it gently and leave in a warm, but not hot, place for 10 minutes until it is bubbling in the jug. Meanwhile dissolve the molasses in a little boiling water and top up with lukewarm water to make 2½ cups (1 pint/600 ml).

Make a well in the middle of the flour mixture and stir the two liquid mixtures in with a large spoon. It will be of a very sloppy consistency. Beat well to make sure that the liquid is distributed to all the flour.

Slowly add some of the remaining flour, continuing to mix. Soon the mixture will become too stiff to stir. Now is the time to get your hands into it. When all the flour has been added work it right to the bottom of the bowl.

Tip the dough on to a floured table top and knead until it becomes even and springy. This will take about 10 minutes. Place the dough back in the bowl, cover with a clean teatowel and leave in a warm (not hot) place for the dough to rise (30–45 minutes).

While waiting for the bread to prove, grease two 2lb (1 kg) or three 1lb (450g) loaf tins. Turn the risen dough out on to the floured board again and knock down. Knead briefly and then cut into 2 or 3 pieces. Knead into a good shape and drop into the tins. Don't be tempted to press it down into the tins – it will fill the corners on its own while rising.

Leave to rise once more for about 20 minutes whilst the oven heats up to 425°F (220°C/Gas Mark 7). As you move your risen bread into the hot oven be very careful that you do not knock the tins. If you do it will collapse and you will have to rise it again. Bake for 40 to 45 minutes.

Remove from the oven and tip one loaf out. While it is still upside down tap it sharply with your fingers. It should make a hollow sound. If not, return to the tin and cook for about 10 minutes longer.

Cool your cooked bread on a wire tray. If you like a softer crust cover it with a teatowel.

Variations: **High protein loaf.** Using the basic recipe given above substitute for the same quantity of flour either 1 cup (4oz/100g) okara or ½ cup (2oz/50g) soya flour. Proceed as above.

Rye bread. Substitute 2 cups (8oz/450g) rye flour for same weight of wholemeal flour in the basic recipe and add 2 teaspoons caraway seeds. Proceed as for basic recipe.

Wholemeal Rolls

Follow the recipe for Sadhya' Bread on page 120. When the dough has proved, knock it down and knead briefly. Divide into three or four pieces and form the pieces into a fat, sausage shape with your hands. Cut small pieces, about the size of a tangerine, and make them into neat ball shapes dusting with flour.

Place them on well greased baking trays, just touching, and allow to rise, covered with a teatowel, for 15 minutes. Preheat the oven to 425°F (220°C/Gas Mark 7) and bake for 20 minutes. They will have joined together while cooking. Tip them all in one piece on to a wire rack and allow to cool before separating.

The rolls can be quickly rewarmed by popping them into a hot oven for 10 minutes to have with soup.

Sourdough Bread

This is an unusual bread with a distinctive flavour because it uses fermenting flour to rise it rather than yeast. You need to make a culture which you feed and then, as it grows, you split it and keep some as a starter for the next batch so you can just keep it going.

It takes a few days to start the culture in the first place but after that you can make your subsequent batches of bread very quickly.

1 **To make the culture**: soak 1 tablespoon of wheat sprouts overnight. Next day drain and rinse. For the next 2 days rinse 2–3 times a day, keeping the grains moist but not flooded. The sprouts should now be showing.

2 Mash the sprouted grain in the blender with 1 cup (8 fl oz/ 250 ml) lukewarm water. Place in a bowl. Add 2 tablespoons of wholemeal flour and stir well with a wooden spoon or chopstick. Cover with a teatowel and leave in a warm place

such as an airing cupboard, above a radiator, or on the stove by the pilot light.

3   Stir twice a day using a wooden implement for 3 days. The mixture should now have begun to ferment. At intervals of several hours add more flour, a dessertspoon at a time, stirring well each time until you have a stiff dough. Leave overnight.

4   **To make the bread**:   put any amount up to 10 times the weight of flour already used (but no more) into a mixing bowl and add the culture. Add lukewarm water about 1¼ cups (½ pint/300 ml) for each 4 cups (1lb/450g) of flour used. Knead to form an elastic dough. Break off a piece of the dough the size of a golf ball and place in a polythene bag in the fridge. This is your next starter. Place the rest of the dough in a bowl, cover, and leave to rise in a warm place for 2½–3 hours.

5   Knock down the risen dough, knead briefly and form into loaves. Place in greased loaf tins and rise again until doubled in size. Preheat the oven to 400°F (200°C/Gas Mark 6) and bake for 10 minutes. Turn down the temperature to 325°F (160°C/ Gas Mark 3) and continue to bake for a further 40–50 minutes, depending on the size of the loaves.

6   **Using your reserved starter**:   mix the piece of reserved dough kept from the previous baking with 1 cup (8 fl oz/250 ml) of lukewarm water, adding a dessertspoon of flour. Keep in a warm place, adding more flour every few hours. There seems no reason to keep it overnight. Continue as from step 4.

Malted Sourdough Bread

Follow the instructions given for Sourdough Bread, but after taking away the golfball-sized piece of dough for your next starter add the following ingredients:

½ to 1 cup (½–1lb/225–
   450g) malt extract
½ cup (4oz/100g) ghee,
   melted
1 cup (6oz/175g) raisins

1 cup (6oz/175g) sultanas
1–2 teaspoons mixed spice
2 teaspoons grated orange
   rind

Knead these ingredients into the dough, adding extra flour to counteract the stickiness of the malt extract and ghee. When well mixed and kneaded place in the mixing bowl and allow to rise for 2 to 3 hours. Continue from step 5 of Sourdough Bread.

Mixed Grain Bread

1½ cups (12 fl oz/350 ml)
boiling water
2 tablespoons ghee
1–2 tablespoons molasses
1 cup (5oz/150g) yellow
cornmeal (polenta)
1 cup (3oz/75g) jumbo oats
1½oz/40g fresh or ½oz/15g
dried yeast

1 cup (8 fl oz/250 ml)
lukewarm water
1 cup (4oz/100g) rye flour
2–3 cups (8–12oz/225–350g)
wholewheat flour (as
needed)

Combine the boiling water, ghee and molasses in a large mixing bowl. Stir in the cornmeal and oats and while this cools to lukewarm combine the yeast with the lukewarm water.

When the yeast mixture is bubbling on top (about 10 minutes), add to the cornmeal mixture in the bowl. Stir in the rye flour and half the wholewheat flour, beating vigorously. Add more wholewheat flour to form a dough which can be turned on to a floured board and kneaded. Knead until elastic and smooth.

Put the dough into an oiled bowl, cover with a cloth and leave in a warm place for about 1½ hours to prove.

When doubled in bulk, turn out once more, punch down and knead briefly. Divide into 2 pieces. Form into rounds and place on a greased and floured baking tray. Cover with a cloth and leave to rise for about 30 minutes. Preheat the oven to 375°F (190°C/Gas Mark 5) and bake for about 45 minutes.

Alternatively, form half the dough into small buns and bake for 20 minutes.

Scones

These fat-free scones are a good alternative to yeast breads. They can be quickly concocted, and you can make them either sweet or savoury.

3 cups (12oz/350g)
    wholewheat flour
1½ cups (12 fl oz/350 ml)
    soya milk or 1½ cups (12 fl
    oz/350 ml) goat's milk
    yoghurt/soya milk mixture

1 teaspoon honey (unset) or
    malt extract

Put the flour into a bowl and make a well in the middle. Pour in the milk, or milk and yoghurt, and the honey or malt extract. Cut through lightly and quickly with a knife until the dough can be turned on to a floured board. Shape into 4 scones. Alternatively, you could lightly roll out to about 1 in (2.5 cm) thickness and cut into small scone shapes with a pastry cutter or an inverted wine glass.

Place on a greased and floured tray. Preheat the oven to 425°F (220°C/Gas Mark 7) for the larger scones or 400°F (200°C/Gas Mark 6) for the smaller scones and bake for 15 minutes.
Variations: add to the uncooked mixture, sliced banana; sultanas; chopped dates; sesame seeds; cinnamon; caraway seeds; chopped onion with a pinch of sage; crushed garlic and pinch of thyme.

Oat Cakes

These are a traditional delicacy from The Potteries. They are a really good substitute for wheat breads. Eat them with salads or soups for lunch or have them for breakfast, warm and spread with a fruit blend. They can be rolled while still hot and filled with either a sweet filling such as fresh fruit, or with a savoury such as hummus or other bean or lentil spread to make a pancake roll.

There are two ways of cooking them shown in the recipe. The pan fried version uses rather a lot of ghee so you should have this only as an occasional treat and use the baked version for more regular use.

1 cup (3oz/75g) fine oatmeal
1 cup (4oz/100g) wholewheat
  flour
1 tablespoon fresh or 1½
  teaspoons dried yeast

1 cup (8 fl oz/250 ml) water
  (warmed)
1½ cups (12 fl oz/350 ml)
  soya milk (warmed)
1 teaspoon malt extract

Mix the oatmeal and flour in a warm basin. Dissolve the yeast in a little of the warm liquids and the malt extract. Set aside in a warm place to rise.

When the yeast has risen mix all the ingredients together and beat to make a good batter. Cover with a clean cloth and leave in a warm place to rise (or if required for breakfast you can leave the batter overnight in the fridge).

Cooking method 1
Melt a small piece of ghee in a frying pan. Spoon as much batter as is required to thinly coat the pan. Allow to cook gently for 3–4 minutes and then with a wooden spatula carefully flip over and cook the other side for a couple of minutes. (I tried to toss these pancakes with rather disastrous results!)

Cooking method 2
Grease a baking tray with a small amount of ghee. Pour the batter on to the tray in small cupfuls and bake at 375°F (190°C/Gas Mark 5) for about 30 minutes until the cakes will lift off easily with a spatula.

Lemon Millet Cake

1 cup (6oz/175g) millet
3 cups (1¼ pints/750 ml)
   apple juice, hot
1 cup (4oz/100g) approx
   cooked grain (rice, oatmeal
   or okara)
1½ cups (6oz/175g)
   wholemeal flour

2 tablespoons (½oz/15g)
   soya flour if available
½ cup (4oz/100g) cashew
   nuts or almonds, roughly
   chopped
2 tablespoons (1oz/25g) ghee,
   melted
grated rind and juice of 1–2
   lemons
2 teaspoons honey

Gently toast the millet in a dry pan for a few minutes. Add the apple juice and bring to the boil. Simmer, covered, for about 20 minutes until cooked and all the liquid is absorbed.

Place the cooked millet in a bowl and add the other ingredients, mixing thoroughly. Place in a greased tin, preheat the oven to 350°F (180°C/Gas Mark 4) and bake for about 1½ hours until firm to the touch.

Fruit Cake

This is a cake that is easy to adapt to whatever you have in your fridge, store cupboard or fruit bowl. It is a good 'use it up' cake; for instance, if you made too much rice last night then you can add some to the cake mix. If you have been making soya milk and have saved the okara then this recipe is a good one to add the okara to. Any home made fruit spreads that haven't been eaten or fruit sauce from breakfast time can go in too. You can be fairly indiscriminate and you will still end up with a good cake. The main thing to remember is to keep the ratio of fruit to grain high, to add grain flour to dry out the mixture if you have used fruit sauce and, most important, when you have achieved the desired consistency, to taste the mixture and decide if it has a good flavour. Things to add to improve the flavour are: grated fresh root ginger, the rind of oranges or lemons, ground cinnamon, molasses, malt extract or perhaps honey, vanilla essence, and carob. Of course you shouldn't add all these to the same cake mix!

2 cups (6oz/175g) jumbo oats
2 cups (8oz/225g) wholemeal flour
1 cup (4oz/100g) approx cooked grain (rice, millet, okara, bulghur wheat etc.)
1 cup (4oz/100g) nuts, (any sort) roughly chopped
1 cup (6oz/175g) raisins, soaked until plump and drained

3 cups (1¼lb/500g) dried fruit (dates, figs, Hunza apricots, soaked and chopped if necessary) or fresh fruit (apple, pear, banana, pineapple, etc., chopped, or grated) or carrot (grated)
½ cup (3½oz/90g) tahini or ghee or creamed coconut desiccated coconut (optional) spices and flavourings to taste

Mix all together, adjusting consistency by adding more flour or desiccated coconut to obtain a thick dryish mixture, and adding spices and flavourings to taste.

Spoon into a greased baking tray and bake at 350°F (180°C/Gas Mark 4) for 1½ to 2 hours until firm to the touch.

Faery Cakes

½ cup (3oz/75g) millet
1 cup (8 fl oz/250 ml) spring water
¼ cup (1oz/25g) creamed coconut, chopped or grated
1½ cups (12 fl oz/350 ml) apple juice

grated rind and juice of 2 lemons
½ cup (6oz/175g) clear honey
¼ cup (1oz/25g) polenta (cornmeal)
½ cup (3oz/75g) sultanas, soaked until plump
extra polenta (optional)

Boil the millet in the spring water with the creamed coconut, stirring frequently (20 minutes). Put the apple juice in a pan with the lemon rind and juice and the honey. Heat to simmer, add the polenta and cook for 5 minutes, stirring gently to prevent lumps. Stir the two mixtures together in a bowl, adding the sultanas. Add a little uncooked polenta meal to make a stiff mixture if necessary.

Place spoonfuls of the mixture in little paper bun cases or into bun trays that have been well greased with ghee. Bake at 375°F (190°C/Gas Mark 5) for about 25 minutes. Alternatively, use a cake tin and bake at 350°F (180°C/Gas Mark 4) for 40 to 50 minutes.

Cornmeal Cake

2 cups (14oz/400g) creamed coconut
6 cups (2½ pints/1.5 litres) soya milk or soya milk and water, hot
few drops real vanilla essence
2 tablespoons honey
2–3 cardamom pods, crushed
1 teaspoon ground cinnamon
2 cups (10oz/275g) yellow cornmeal (polenta)
1–2 bananas, sliced
½ cup (3oz/75g) raisins, soaked for 1 hour until plump

Melt the creamed coconut in the heated soya milk. Add the vanilla essence, honey, cardamom pods and cinnamon.

Stir in the cornmeal and add the sliced bananas and the raisins. Place in a greased baking tray and bake at 375°F (190°C/Gas Mark 5) for about 1 hour.

Variation: this cake is also delicious in a lemon version. Add the grated rind and juice of 2 lemons to the liquid and continue as above.

JAMS AND SPREADS

Here are a number of ideas for spreads which you can use either on bread or toast or as a filling for cakes. As they are not made using sugar, they will not keep like a commercial jam. Make only enough for a day or two and keep in the fridge.

Orange Jam

Soak a few figs overnight. Blend, adding lemon juice, the grated rind of an orange and sufficient ground cashew nuts to form a thick paste.

Mulberry and Apple Jam

Chop 1–2 apples and discard the cores. Place in the blender with a handful of dried mulberries and a little apple juice. Blend well and adjust the consistency by adding either more mulberries if too runny or apple juice if too thick.

Carob Nut Spread

Blend a handful of sultanas with a little soya milk. Add ½ teaspoon carob and sufficient ground hazelnuts to form a paste. This spread is extra delicious if you lightly toast the nuts before grinding.

Apricot Jam

Soak Hunza apricots overnight. Remove the stones. Blend the fruit with ground cashew nuts, adding the apricot soaking juice to achieve the correct consistency. A little lemon juice and grated rind can be included if you like.

Fig Marmalade

Chop figs into small pieces and simmer in a little water. Blend with the flesh of 1–2 oranges (blood oranges look amazing) and the grated rind of 1 orange. Thicken with ground almonds.

Nut Butter

Lightly toast a mixture of nuts. We like almonds with hazelnuts and sunflower seeds. Grind together, adding a little sunflower oil to bind. This butter will keep in the fridge for about a week.

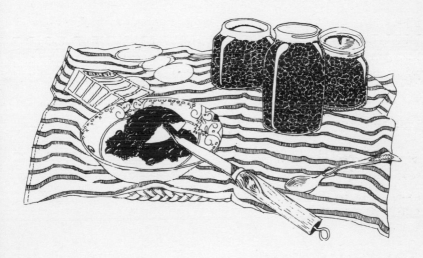

8
Chutneys and Sauces

These will liven up a simple dish with their sharp, fruity taste. They are very simple to concoct and, because they contain vinegar, will keep for a number of days in the fridge.

When you have made them a few times you will be able to improvise and make your own versions, using whatever is available in your kitchen.

C.H.C. Brown Sauce

4 tomatoes, chopped
½ cup (3oz/75g) dates, chopped small and soaked in cider vinegar
½ cup (4 fl oz/120 ml) cider vinegar
1–2 apples, chopped

1–2 onions, chopped
1 clove garlic, crushed
1 teaspoon garam masala
1 teaspoon molasses (or to taste)
apple juice as needed

Blend all together, adding a little water or apple juice to adjust the consistency.

Apricot Chutney

1 cup (6oz/175g) Hunza apricots, soaked overnight and stoned
1–2 onions, finely chopped
1 cup (6oz/175g) dates, chopped small and soaked in apple juice

½ cup (3oz/175g) sultanas
1–2 cloves garlic, crushed
1 teaspoon ground coriander
1 teaspoon ground cinnamon
apple juice as needed
cider vinegar as needed

Blend half the apricots with the soaking water, half the onions and half the dates.

Chop the rest of the apricots up fairly small and combine with the rest of the dates and onions along with the sultanas, garlic and spices.

Apple Chutney

1 cup (6oz/175g) dates,
   soaked overnight in cider
   vinegar
apple juice as required
2–3 apples, finely chopped
1–2 onions, very finely
   chopped

1 cup (6oz/175g) sultanas
small piece of fresh root
   ginger, grated
malt extract to taste
cider vinegar as required

Blend the dates in the cider vinegar in which they soaked, adding apple juice if necessary. Add half the apples and half the onions and blend.

Mix with the other ingredients, adding cider vinegar and apple juice to adjust the flavour and consistency.

Orange and Ginger Sauce

4 oranges
2 onions, roughly chopped
½ cup (3oz/75g) sultanas
1 apple, roughly chopped

piece of fresh root ginger,
   grated
cider vinegar as needed

Grate the rind of one of the oranges. Peel all the oranges and place in the blender with the grated rind and all the other ingredients except the cider vinegar. Blend and add cider vinegar to taste.

9
Drinks

If you have a lifetime's coffee and tea drinking behind you, don't despair. Of course it will take a while to forget the habit completely but the addiction and mild craving will pass in a week or two and you will soon appreciate the wholesomeness of the alternatives. Fruit and vegetable juices don't give you a quick 'high' followed shortly by a 'low' that makes you crave another cup, nor will they make you jittery or keep you awake at night like coffee and tea do. They are really good for you – fruit and vegetable juices are absolutely packed with vitamins and minerals (and carrot juice is an acknowledged cancer treatment). Herb teas not only have lovely delicate flavours and are very refreshing, they also have properties of a medicinal kind. Some aid the digestion, some are calmative, others are very cleansing. There are some interesting books available on the medicinal properties of herbs and this can be a whole study in itself. I shall only talk about them here in terms of a refreshing drink. There is such a variety of good and wholesome drinks available to you on this diet that soon you will forget about your old habits.

Juices

If you have a juicing machine it is easy to make vegetable and fruit juices (a blender will not do this). The fruits and vegetables are simply prepared by washing and cutting to size to fit your machine. Then, with the motor running, you push the vegetables or fruit through. In some models the juice is expressed into another compartment, in others you place a glass below the spout. Usually the pulp is left in the centrifugal drum. If you like to be super-economical you can add this pulp to dishes such as cakes, crumbles and burgers, but with an efficient machine only the fibre is left behind and on this diet you are certainly not going to be short on fibre.

As well as making juices from individual fruit and vegetables you can also make cocktails. Some vegetables have a very strong flavour but it's good to add a little with a milder vegetable. You may be surprised at how good combinations of fruit and vegetables are.

1   1 part carrot juice: 1 part apple juice

2   2 parts carrot juice: 1 part orange juice

3   1 part beetroot juice: 2 parts pineapple juice

4   1 part beetroot juice: 2 parts grape juice

5   2 parts carrot juice: 2 parts tomato juice: 1 part cabbage juice: 1 part beetroot juice: 1 part watercress juice

6   2 parts carrot juice: 2 parts celery juice: 2 parts lettuce juice: 1 part tomato juice: 1 part apple juice

7   2 parts carrot juice: 1 part alfalfa sprout juice: 1 part pear juice: 1 part spring onion juice

As you will notice, I have included alfalfa sprouts in one of the combinations. Other sprouts that go well in these juices are lentil sprouts and mung bean sprouts. These are just a few combination ideas. Experiment and discover your own favourites.

You may find that your stomach is a little surprised to receive all these vegetables without the fibre. To help it with the digestion, always sip your juices rather than gulping them down. Give the saliva in the mouth a chance to do its job in the digestive process.

Good combinations for purely fruit juices are: apple and pear; apple and grape; grape and melon; and pineapple and gooseberry.

As you see there is no limit to the combinations and I'm sure you will enjoy trying lots of mixes using the fruits and vegetables in season.

Carrot Juice

All patients staying with us at the centre in Bristol are offered a glass of carrot juice each day. We use it as part of our treatment as it has been shown that a low intake of vitamin A and of betacarotene is associated with the occurrence of cancer. Although the amount of carrot juice to take will vary patient to patient, most people can take three tumblers of carrot juice daily. If the making of this juice is difficult to fit into your lifestyle, or if you have difficulty obtaining organic carrots in this quantity (and for this concentration of juice, it is very important to use only organic) then betacarotene tablets are available. Some people find it convenient to take the betacarotene tablets while they are out at work all day and then to drink a fresh carrot juice in the evening.

To prepare carrot juice: take 4–5 organically grown carrots, wash and brush them well but do not scrape or peel them. Put through your juicer to give 1 cup (8 fl oz/250 ml) of juice. Emulsify with ½ teaspoon cold pressed sunflower oil. This is best done in a blender, although it is possible to use a rotary whisk. You will see when it is properly emulsified as the colour will change from a deep blood red to a light orange. This will take about 1½ minutes in a blender and a little longer with a whisk. The reason for the oil is to make it more digestible. Drink immediately.

Herb Teas

If you have herbs growing in your garden or in pots on the patio or balcony then your herb teas are waiting to be picked.

Just cut a few sprigs, place in a jug and pour boiling water over. Allow to infuse for about 5 minutes, then strain into a cup. A slice of lemon may be added if you wish. On hot summer days it's good to keep a jug of herb tea (strained) in the fridge as you will find this very refreshing.

There are now lots of commercial herb tea bags on the market and all wholefood shops stock a good range. They are quick and easy to use although a little expensive. You will find mixed herb tea bags with well-balanced combinations of herbs. On the other hand it is much cheaper to buy your favourite herbs loose and to experiment with your own mixtures. You will need about 1 teaspoon of herbs to about 2½ cups (1 pint/600 ml) boiling water, to make 2 cups. Infuse for about 5 minutes and strain.

Here is a list of the herbs we enjoy drinking, either on their own or in combination: peppermint, lemon balm, chamomile, fennel, sage, lime flower (linden blossom), rosehip, hibiscus, nettle. If you enjoy the flavour of ginger then you can add a small piece of fresh root ginger to the jug.

High Protein Drinks

There are various times when these high protein drinks can be extremely useful, for example as a quick nourishing snack in the middle of a busy day when there is not time to prepare a full meal, or perhaps as a very quick breakfast. More importantly, if you have lost weight following surgery and are feeling frail and run down these drinks will help you to gain weight and strength. Sometimes at the beginning of this diet it is difficult for the body to adapt immediately to this 'new' food and you may find that to start with you can't actually eat enough of this sort of food to maintain weight. If your cancer is associated with the digestive tract you may have difficulty in absorbing the nutrients that are needed to make a healthy diet. Under all these circumstances these high protein drinks are of great value.

In the recipes that follow all the drinks can be thinned down to the desired consistency with either spring water or fruit juice.

Almond Cream

1 tablespoon almonds, ground
1 apricot kernel, ground (optional)

½ cup (4 fl oz/120 ml) soya milk
½ cup (4 fl oz/120 ml) spring water
1 teaspoon malt extract

Blend them all together.

Apricot Delight

5 Hunza apricots, soaked and stoned
1 cup (8 fl oz/250 ml) Hunza juice (the liquid in which they were soaked)

¼ cup (1½oz/40g) tofu
1 tablespoon cooked rice or other grain

Blend together.

Summer Drink

½ cup (2oz/50g) soft fruit such as strawberries or raspberries
1 tablespoon cashew nuts, ground

½ cup (4 fl oz/120 ml) soya milk
1 tablespoon oat flakes

Blend them all together.

Figgy Drink

1 apple, cored
2–3 figs, soaked and chopped

fig soaking juice
1 cup (8 fl oz/250 ml) soya
   milk

Blend until smooth.

Tofu Fruit Drink

¼ cup (1½oz/40g) tofu
1 tablespoon cooked grain
   (rice, millet, barley)
1 ripe banana

½ cup (4 fl oz/120 ml) soya
   milk
juice of ½ lemon

Blend all together.

Orange Cream

juice of 2–3 oranges
¼ cup (1½oz/40g) tofu

¼ cup (1oz/25g) cashew
   nuts, ground
a little spring water

Blend all together.

Pear Cream

1–2 ripe pears, chopped
1 tablespoon almonds,
   ground

½ cup (4 fl oz/120 ml)
   spring water
pinch of ground cinnamon

Blend all together.

Mint Julep

1 cup (8 fl oz/250 ml) apple   *1 teaspoon oatflakes*
   juice   *sprig of mint*
¼ cup (1½oz/40g) tofu

Blend all together and serve decorated with a mint leaf.

10
Oven Temperatures

Description	Fahrenheit	Centigrade	Gas mark
Cool	225	110	¼
Very Slow	275	140	1
Slow	325	160	3
Moderate	350	180	4
Moderately Hot	400	200	6
Hot	450	230	8
Very Hot	475	240	9

11
Recommended Reading

The Bean Book, Rose Elliot (Fontana, 1979)

Not Just A Load Of Old Lentils, Rose Elliot (Fontana, 1976)

Raw Energy, Leslie and Susannah Kenton (Century, 1984)

Diet For A Small Planet, Frances Moore Lappe (Ballantine, New York, 1975)

Recipes for a Small Planet, Ellen Buchman Ewald (Ballantine, New York, 1973)

Making Your Own Home Proteins, Evelyn Findlater (Century, 1985)

The Book of Tofu, W. Shurtleff & A. Aoyagi (Ballantine, New York, 1979)

Organic Gardening, Lawrence D. Hills (Penguin, 1977)

Index

There is a tape available from the Cancer Help Centre with meditation and visualisation techniques that can be used alongside any kind of cancer therapy. If you would like a copy of 'Helping with Healing' please send £5 (V.A.T. and p & p inclusive) per copy with this order form.

To: Cancer Help Centre, Bristol
Grove House
Cornwallis Grove
Clifton
Bristol BS8 4PG
(Tel. 0272 – 743216)

Please send .... copy/s of 'Helping with Healing'.

I enclose £............ cash/cheque/Barclaycard/Access/Visa

NAME: ....

Address ....

....

....

....

Signature ....

Access/Visa/Barclaycard No ....